ARCHETYPAL PSYCHOLOGY

A Brief Account

Archetypal Psychology

A Brief Account

Together with a Complete Checklist of Works

by

James Hillman

Spring Publications, Inc.
Woodstock, Connecticut

Originally published in Italian as
"Psicologia archetipica" a chapter
in Volume V of *Enciclopedia del Novecento*, 1981

Published by Spring Publications, Inc.,
299 East Quassett Road,
Woodstock, Connecticut, 06281
E-mail Spring@neca.com
Printed in the province of Québec, Canada
Text printed on acidfree paper.
Cover designed and produced by
Catherine Meehan and Sven Doehner

Library of Congress Cataloging in Publication Data
Hillman, James.
Archetypal psychology : a brief account.
Bibliography: p.
　1. Archetype (Psychology) 2. Psychoanalysis.
I. Title.
BF175.H458　　　1983　　　150.19'54　　　82—19663
ISBN 0—88214—373—5

 PRINTED IN CANADA

Contents

*tanti ringraziamenti a Bianca Garufi
ed ai miei amici italiani*

Foreword

This monograph was written during the Autumn of 1979 at the request of the Istituto dell'Enciclopedia Italiana for inclusion in Volume V (813-21) of the *Enciclopedia del Novecento*, published in 1981, where it can be read in the Italian translation of Bianca Garufi. Her assiduous attention helped these condensed formulations find their final expression.

Though I feel ambivalent about these sorts of abbreviations, it seemed to me that since it was out in translation why not in the original. For this first publication in English, I have made scarcely any revisions, neither bringing the literature up-to-date (other than a few insertions), nor enumerating the directions archetypal psychology has taken in various hands since 1979, nor reporting on lectures, conferences, meetings. Developments move so quickly that the fantasy of "keeping-up-to-date" is misplaced. Rather, this essay serves merely to locate archetypal psychology as a topic of thought presented in the style of an encyclopedia of the twentieth century.

To supplement this monograph with its own full bibliography, there is appended a complete checklist of my writings, including translations and unpublished papers, which replaces and extends the one concluding in 1975 that was available in *Loose Ends*.

I am extremely grateful to Robert Scott Dupree for his masterful work with the checklist, to Susan Dupree who expertly and caringly composed the text, and to Mary Helen Gray for supervising the editing and production of the entire work. She made this book.

Dallas, October 1982

J. H.

Prefatory Note to the Fifth Printing

We have again revised the checklist of publications comprising Part Three of this little book, adding entries since the 1988 edition and completing it into January 1993. As well, translations and cross-references have been collated with the original versions so that, as best as we know, this checklist is correct and thorough. The job took several fine hands: Pierre Denivelle, Mary Helen (Gray) Sullivan, Jacob Rabinowitz, and especially A. K. O Donoghue with whom I have worked on bibliographies, translations, and references since the late 1950s. I am glad to thank them each for their diligent care.

To revise, however, Parts One and Two of this little book is beyond anyone's reach, since the field called archetypal psychology continues to extend so widely, and wildly. This proliferation of ideas and works was exemplified at the Festival of Archetypal Psychology at the University of Notre Dame, Indiana (July 1992). Attended by nearly five hundred people, the event lasted six days and was the occasion for papers, lectures, poetry, exhibitions, performances, films, and discussions by men and women from many parts of the world whose work directly or tangentially affects, or is affected by, the ideas summarized in this little book. To include the work of the nineties and the elaborations of the eighties goes beyond the intention of "A Brief Account," which this book purports to be.

Nonetheless, readers might like to know of five periodicals that present the movement of ideas in the field: *Gorgo: Zeitschrift fur archetypische Psychologie und bildhaftes Denken*, Zürich: Schweizer Spiegel Verlag; *Anima*, Casella postale 93, 50012 Bagno a Ripoli, Firenze; *L'immaginale*, Casella postale 273, 73100 Lecce; *Sphinx*, Box 417, London NW3 6YE; and, of course, *Spring: A Journal of Archetype and Culture*, which now appears twice a year and can be ordered from Spring Publications.

February 28, 1993   J. H.

Part One

1   Sources of Archetypal Psychology

Archetypal psychology, first named as such by James Hillman (1970b), had from its beginning the intention of moving beyond clinical inquiry within the consulting room of psychotherapy by situating itself within the culture of Western imagination. It is a psychology deliberately affiliated with the arts, culture, and the history of ideas, arising as they do from the imagination. The term "archetypal," in contrast to "analytical" which is the usual appellation for C. G. Jung's psychology, was preferred not only because it reflected "the deepened theory of Jung's later work which attempts to solve psychological problems beyond scientific models" (Hillman 1970b); it was preferred more importantly because "archetypal" belongs to all culture, all forms of human activity, and not only to professional practitioners of modern therapeutics. By traditional definition, archetypes are the primary forms that govern the psyche. But they cannot be contained only by the psyche, since they manifest as well in physical, social, linguistic, aesthetic, and spiritual modes. Thus archetypal psychology's first links are with culture and imagination rather than with medical and empirical psychologies, which tend to confine psychology to the positivistic manifestations of the nineteenth-century condition of the soul.

Archetypal psychology can be seen as a cultural movement part of whose task is the re-visioning of psychology,
psychopathology, and psychotherapy in terms of the Western
cultural imagination. In an early review of the field and an examination of its main thrusts, Goldenberg (1975) regards
archetypal psychology as a "third generation" derivative of the
Jungian school in which Jung is recognized as the source but
not as the doctrine. Two themes of its directions which she
singles out—the emphasis upon psychopathology and the radical relativization and desubstantiation of the ego—will be
discussed below.

It is without doubt that the first immediate father of
archetypal psychology is Carl Gustav Jung, the Swiss psychologist (1875–1961). James Hillman, Raphael Lopez–Pedraza,
Patricia Berry, Paul Kugler, Murray Stein, Adolf
Guggenbühl–Craig, Bianca Garufi, Robert Grinnell, and
many others of the authors referred to below were trained
as Jungian analysts. (However, a significant number of other
authors to be mentioned —e.g., David Miller, Edward Casey,
Gilbert Durand, Mary Watkins, Robert Sardello, Charles
Boer—did not receive this specific Jungian formation and
contribute to archetypal psychology from phenomenology,
literature, poetry, philosophy, religious studies, etc.) From
Jung comes the idea that the basic and universal structures
of the psyche, the formal patterns of its relational modes,
are archetypal patterns. These are like psychic organs, con-
genitally given with the psyche (yet not necessarily genetically
inherited), even if somewhat modified by historical and geographical factors. These patterns or *archai* appear in the arts,
religions, dreams, and social customs of all peoples, and they
manifest spontaneously in mental disorders. For Jung, they are

anthropological and cultural, and also spiritual in that they tran-
scend the empirical world of time and place, and in fact, are in
themselves not phenomenal. Archetypal psychology, in distinction to Jungian, considers the archetypal to be always
phenomenal (Avens 1980), thus avoiding the Kantian idealism
implied in Jung (de Voogd 1977).

The primary and irreducible language of these archetypal patterns is the metaphorical discourse of myths.
These can therefore be understood as the most fundamental
patterns of human existence. To study human nature at its
most basic level, one must turn to culture (mythology, religion, art, architecture, epic, drama, ritual) where these
patterns are portrayed. The full implication of this move
away from biochemical, socio-historical, and personal-be-
havioristic bases for human nature and toward the
imaginative has been articulated by Hillman as "the poetic
basis of mind" (q.v.). Support for the archetypal and psychological significance of myth, besides the work of Jung,
comes from Ernst Cassirer, Karl Kerényi, Erich Neumann,
Heinrich Zimmer, Gilbert Durand, Joseph Campbell, David
Miller, and Charles Boer.

The second immediate father of archetypal psychology
is Henry Corbin (1903–1978), the French scholar, philosopher,
and mystic, principally known for his interpretation of Islamic
thought. From Corbin (1971–73) comes the idea that the *mundus
archetypalis* (*'alam al-mithal*) is also the *mundus imaginalis*. It
is a distinct field of imaginal realities requiring methods and
perceptual faculties different from the spiritual world beyond it
or the empirical world of usual sense perception and naive formulation. The *mundus imaginalis* offers an ontological mode
of locating the archetypes of the psyche as the fundamental

structures of the imagination or as fundamentally imaginative
phenomena that are transcendent to the world of sense in their
value if not their appearance. Their value lies in their theophanic
nature and in their virtuality or potentiality which is always
ontologically more than actuality and its limits. (As phenomena
they must appear, though this appearance is to the imagination
or in the imagination.) The *mundus imaginalis* provides for
archetypes a valuative and cosmic grounding, when this is
needed, different from such bases as biological instinct, eternal
forms, numbers, linguistic and social transmission, biochemical
reactions, genetic coding, etc.

   But more important than the ontological placing of
archetypal realities is the double move of Corbin: (a) that
the fundamental nature of the archetype is accessible to
imagination first, and first presents itself as image so that
(b) the entire procedure of archetypal psychology as a
method is imaginative. Its exposition must be rhetorical and
poetic, its reasoning not logical, and its therapeutic aim neither
social adaptation nor personalistic individualizing but rather
a work in service of restoration of the patient to imaginal
realities. The aim of therapy (q.v.) is the development of a
sense of soul, the middle ground of psychic realities, and
the method of therapy is the cultivation of imagination.

   In extending the tradition of Jung and Corbin forward,
archetypal psychology has had to go back to their prede-
cessors, particularly the Neoplatonic tradition of Vico and
the Renaissance, through Proclus and Plotinus, to Plato
(*Phaedo, Phaedrus, Symposium, Timaeus*), and most an-
ciently to Heraclitus. (Corbin's works on Avicenna, Ibn'
Arabi, and Sohrawardi belong also in this tradition as does
the work of Kathleen Raine on William Blake [1758–1835]

and on Thomas Taylor, the English translator of the main writings of Plato and the Neoplatonists.)

The elaboration of this tradition by Hillman in Eranos lectures and in articles (1973a), by Miller in seminars at Syracuse University, by Lopez–Pedraza at the University of Caracas, and by Thomas Moore's (1982) and Boer's (1980) work on Marsilio Ficino gives a different cast to archetypal psychology when compared with Jung's. There the background is more German (Nietzsche, Schopenhauer, Carus, von Hartmann, Kant, Goethe, Eckhart, and Bohme), Christian, psychiatric, and Eastern. Archetypal psychology situates itself more comfortably *south* (q.v.) of the Alps.

Especially—this Neoplatonic tradition is thoroughly Western even if it is not empirical in method, rationalist in conception, or otherworldly spiritual in appeal. This tradition holds to the notion of soul as a first principle, placing this soul as a *tertium* between the perspectives of body (matter, nature, empirics) and of mind (spirit, logic, idea). Soul as the *tertium*, the perspective *between* others and from which others may be viewed, has been described as Hermetic consciousness (Lopez–Pedraza 1977), as *"esse in anima"* (Jung [1921] *CW 6*, §66, 77), as the position of the *mundus imaginalis* by Corbin, and by Neoplatonic writers on the intermediaries or figures of the *metaxy*. Body, soul, spirit: this tripartite anthropology further separates archetypal psychology from the usual Western dualistic division, whose history goes back before Descartes to at least the ninth century (869: Eighth General Council at Constantinople), occurring also in the medieval ascension of Averroes' Aristotelianism over Avicenna's Platonism. Consequences of this dualistic division are still being felt in that the psyche has become indistinguishable from bodily life, on the one hand, or from the life of the spirit on the other. In the dualistic tradition, psyche never had its own logos. There could be no true psychology. A first methodologically consistent attempt to articulate one in a *philosophical* style belongs also within the perimeters of archetypal psychology (Evangelos Christou 1963).

2   *Image and Soul: The Poetic Basis of Mind*

The *datum* with which archetypal psychology begins is the image. The image was identified with the psyche by Jung ("image is psyche"—*CW 13*, §75), a maxim which archetypal psychology has elaborated to mean that the soul is constituted of images, that the soul is primarily an imagining activity most natively and paradigmatically presented by the dream. For it is in the dream that the dreamer performs as one image among others and where it can legitimately be shown that the dreamer is in the image rather than the image in the dreamer.

The source of images—dream-images, fantasy-images, poetic-images—is the self-generative activity of the soul. In archetypal psychology the word "image," therefore, does not refer to an after-image, the result of sensations and perceptions; nor does "image" mean a mental construct that represents in symbolic form certain ideas and feelings which it expresses. In fact the image has no referent beyond itself, neither proprioceptive, external, nor semantic: "images don't stand for anything" (Hillman 1978a). They are the psyche in its imaginative visibility; as primary *datum*, image is irreducible. (The relation of image and "structure" has been discussed by Patricia Berry 1974 and by Paul Kugler 1979b.)

Visibility, however, need not mean that an image must be visually seen. It does not have to have hallucinatory properties which confuse the act of perceiving images with imagining them. Nor do images have to be heard as in a poetic passage. Such notions of "visibility" tend to literalize images as distinct events presented to the senses. Hence Casey (1974) in his path-breaking essay, "Toward an Archetypal Imagination," states that an image is not what one sees but the way in which one sees. An image is given by the imagining perspective and can only be perceived by an act of imagining.

The autochthonous quality of images as *independent* (Watkins 1981, 24f.) of the subjective imagination which does the perceiving takes Casey's idea one step further. *First*, one believes images are hallucinations (things seen); *then* one recognizes them as acts of subjective imagining; but then, *third*, comes the awareness that images are independent of subjectivity and even of the imagination itself as a mental activity. Images come and go (as in dreams) at their own will, with their own rhythm, within their own fields of relations, undetermined by personal psychodynamics. In fact images are the fundamentals which make the movements of psychodynamics possible. They claim reality; that is, authority, objectivity, and certainty. In this third recognition, the mind is in the imagination rather than the imagination in the mind. The noetic and the imaginal no longer oppose each other

(Hillman 1981a, b). "Yet this is still 'psychology' although no longer science; it is psychology in the wider meaning of the word, a psychological activity of creative nature, in which creative fantasy is given prior place" (Jung, *CW* 6, §84).

Corbin (1958) attributes this recognition to the awakened heart as *locus* of imagining, a *locus* also familiar in the Western tradition from Michelangelo's *immagine del cuor*. This interdependence of heart and image intimately ties the basis of archetypal psychology with the phenomena of love (q.v. eros). Corbin's theory of creative imagination of the heart further implies for psychology that, when it bases itself in the image, it must at the same time recognize that imagination is not merely a human faculty but is an activity of soul to which the human imagination bears witness. It is not we who imagine but we who are imagined.

When "image" is thus transposed from a human representation of its conditions to a *sui generis* activity of soul in independent presentation of its bare nature, all empirical studies on imagination, dream, fantasy, and the creative process in artists, as well as methods of *rêve dirigé*, will contribute little to a psychology of the image if they start with the empirics of imagining rather than with the phenomenon of the image—which is not a product of imagining. Empirical approaches of analyzing and guiding images strive to gain control over them. Archetypal psychology distinguishes itself radically from these methods of image control as has been argued by Watkins (1976, 1981). Casey's turning of the notion of image from something seen to a way of seeing (a seeing of the heart—Corbin) offers archetypal psychology's solution to an old dilemma between true (*vera*) imagination

(Paracelsus) and false, or fancy (Coleridge). For archetypal psychology, the distinction depends upon the way in which the image is responded to and worked. The criteria it uses, therefore, refer to *response*: metaphorical and imaginative as being a better response than fanciful or literal, and this because, where the former response is "fecund" (Langer), furthering the deepening and elaboration of the image, the latter responses dissipate or program the image into more naive, shallow, or fixedly dogmatic significance.

     For archetypal psychology, images are neither good nor bad, true nor false, demonic nor angelic (Hillman 1977a), though an image always implicates "a precisely qualified context, mood and scene" (as Hillman [1977b] has on one occasion defined the image). Thus they do invite judgment as a further precision of the image; judgment arising from the image as an effect of the image's own presentation of a claim for response. Therefore to suspend judgment is to fall into the objectivist fantasy. Judgments are inherent to the image (as a work of art brings with it the standards by which it can be measured or a text brings with it the hermeneutics by which it can be interpreted). Archetypal psychology examines the judgments about the image imagistically, regarding them as its further specifications and as psychological statements not to be taken literally from a spiritual (q.v.), purely noetic, vantage point detached from the context of the image judged.

     The emphasis upon response has led archetypal psychology to use the analogy of the craftsman when discussing moral judgments. How well has the image worked; does the image release and refine further imagining? Does the response "stick to the image" (Lopez–Pedraza) as the task at hand, rather than associate or amplify into non-imagistic symbolisms, personal opinions, and interpretations? Such are the questions asked by archetypal psychology.

"Stick to the image" (cf. Jung, *CW* 16, §320) has become a golden rule of archetypal psychology's method, and this because the image is the primary psychological *datum*. Though the image implies more than it presents, "the depth of the image—its limitless ambiguities . . . can only be partly grasped as implications. So to expand upon the dream image is also to narrow it—a further reason we wish never to stray too far from the source" (Berry 1974, 98).

It must be noted that the "source" is *complex*; archetypal psychology is complex at the beginning, since the image is a self-limiting, multiple relationship of meanings, moods, historical events, qualitative details, and expressive possibilities. As its referent is imaginal, it always retains a virtuality beyond its actuality (Corbin 1977, 167). An image always seems more profound (archetypal), more powerful (potential), and more beautiful (theophanic) than the comprehension of it; hence the feeling, while recording a dream, of seeing through a glass darkly. Hence, too, the driving necessity in the arts, for they provide complicated disciplines that can actualize the complex virtuality of the image.

This polysemous complexity bespeaks a polytheistic (q.v.) psychology of personifications analogous with Jung's theory of complexes as the multiple consciousness at the base of psychic life (*CW* 8, §388ff.). By starting with a complex *datum*—the image—archetypal psychology is saved from accounting for psychic life in simplistic terms of elementary mechanisms, primordialities of origins, or numerically limited basic structures. Reductionism is defeated from the start, because the mind is poetic to begin with, and consciousness is not a later, secondary elaboration upon a primitive base but is given with that base in each image.

The "poetic basis of mind" was a thesis Hillman (1975a, xi) first set forth in his 1972 Terry Lectures at Yale University. It states that archetypal psychology "starts neither in the physiology of the brain, the structure of language, the organization of society, nor the analysis of behavior, but in processes of imagination." The inherent relation between psychology and the cultural imagination is necessitated by the nature of mind. The most fecund approach to the study of mind is thus through its highest imaginational responses (Hough 1973; Giegerich 1982; Berry 1982) where the images are most fully released and elaborated.

3   Archetypal Image

Archetypal psychology *axiomatically* assumes imagistic universals, comparable to the *universali fantastici* of Vico (S.N. II, I, 1:381), that is, mythical figures that provide the poetic characteristics of human thought, feeling, and action, as well as the physiognomic intelligibility of the qualitative worlds of natural phenomena. By means of the archetypal image, natural phenomena present faces that speak to the imagining soul rather than only conceal hidden laws and probabilities and manifest their objectification.

A psychological universal must be considered *psychologically*. An archetypal image is psychologically "universal" because its effect amplifies and de-personalizes.

Even if the notion of image (q.v.) regards each image as an individualized, unique event, as "that image there and no other," such an image is universal because it resonates with collective, trans-empirical importance. Thus, archetypal psychology uses "universal" as an adjective, declaring a substantive perduring *value* which ontology states as a hypostasis. And the universals problem for psychology is not whether they exist, where, and how they participate in particulars, but rather whether a personal individual event can be recognized as bearing essential and collective importance. Psychologically the universals problem is presented by the soul whose perspective is harmoniously both the narrow particularity of felt experience and the universality of archetypally human experience. In Neoplatonic thought, soul could be spoken of as both my soul and world soul, and what was true of one was true of both. Thus the universality of an archetypal image means also that the response to the image implies more than personal consequences, raising the soul beyond its egocentric confines (q.v. soul–making) and broadening the events of nature from discrete atomic particulars to aesthetic signatures bearing information for soul.

Because archetypal psychology gives priority to particular pattern over literal particle—and considers that particular events are always themselves imagistic and therefore ensouled—imagination too is assumed to be primordially patterned into typical themes, motifs, regions, genres, and syndromes. These kinds of patterns inform all psychic life. Gilbert Durand (1960, 1979)—following upon the lines opened by Bachelard—and Durand's *centre de recherche sur l'imaginaire* at Chambery, have been charting the inherent organization of the imaginary as the basis of cultural anthropology and sociology, even as the basis of psychological meaning in consciousness. Durand's papers published in the *Eranos Yearbooks* since 1964 present a range of archetypal cultural analysis.

Archetypal psychology has pressed beyond the collection of objective data and the correlation of images as verbal or visual symbols. If archetypal images are the fundamentals of fantasy, they are the means by which the world is imagined, and therefore they are the models by which all knowledge, all experiences whatsoever become possible. "Every psychic process is an image and an "imagining," otherwise no consciousness could exist . . . " (*CW* 11, §889). An archetypal image operates like the original meaning of idea (from Greek *eidos* and *eidolon*): not only "that which" one sees but also that "by means of which" one sees. The demonstration of archetypal images is therefore as much in the act of seeing as in the object seen, since the archetypal image appears in consciousness as the governing fantasy by means of which consciousness is possible to begin with. Gathering of data does less to demonstrate objectively the existence of archetypes than it does to demonstrate the fantasy of "objective data."

Furthermore, unlike Jung, who radically distinguishes between noumenal archetype *per se* and phenomenal archetypal image, archetypal psychology rigorously refuses even to speculate about a non-presented archetype *per se*. Its concern is with the phenomenon: the archetypal image. This leads to the next step: ". . . any image can be considered archetypal. The word 'archetypal'. . . rather than pointing at something archetypal points to something, and this is *value* . . . by archetypal psychology we mean a psychology of value. And our appellative move is aimed to

restore psychology to its widest, richest and deepest volume
so that it would resonate with soul [q.v.] in its descriptions
as unfathomable, multiple, prior, generative, and necessary.
As all images can gain this archetypal sense, so all psychology
can be archetypal . . . 'Archetypal' here refers to a move one
makes rather than to a thing that is" (Hillman 1977b, 82-83).

Here, archetypal psychology "sees through" itself as
strictly a psychology of archetypes, a mere analysis of structures of being (Gods in their myths), and, by emphasizing
the valuative function of the adjective "archetypal," restores
to images their primordial place as that which gives psychic
value to the world. Any image termed "archetypal" is im-
mediately valued as universal, trans-historical, basically
profound, generative, highly intentional, and necessary.

Since "archetypal" connotes both intentional force
(Jung's "instinct") and the mythical field of personifications
(Hillman's "Gods"), an archetypal image is animated like
an animal (one of Hillman's frequent metaphors for images)
and like a person whom one loves, fears, delights in, is in-
hibited by, and so forth. As intentional force and person,
such an image presents a claim—moral, erotic, intellectual,
aesthetic—and demands a response. It is an "affecting presence" (Armstrong 1971) offering an affective relationship.
It seems to bear prior knowledge (coded information) and
an instinctive direction for a destiny, as if prophetic, or prog-
nostic. Images in "dreams mean well for us, back us up and
urge us on, understand us more deeply than we understand
ourselves, expand our sensuousness and spirit, continually
make up new things to give us—and this feeling of being
loved by the images . . . call it imaginal love" (Hillman
1979a, 196). This message bearing experience of the image—

and the feeling of blessing that an image can bring—recalls the Neoplatonic sense of images as daimones and angels (message bearers). "Perhaps—who knows?—these eternal images are what men mean by fate" (_CW_ 7, §183).

Although an archetypal image presents itself as impacted with meaning, this is not given simply as revelation. It must be _made_ through "image work" and "dream work" (Hillman 1977b, 1979a). The modes of this work may be concrete and physical as in art, movement, play, and occupational therapies. But more importantly, because less fixedly symbolic, this work is done by "sticking to the image" as a psychological penetration of what is actually presented including the stance of consciousness that is attempting the hermeneutic. Image work is not legitimately such unless the implicit involvement of a subjective perspective is admitted from the start, for it too is part of the image and in its fantasy.

Image work requires both aesthetic culture and a background in myths and symbols for appreciation of the universalities of images. This work also requires a series of tactical moves (Hillman and Berry 1977), frequently linguistic and phonetic (Sardello et al. 1978; Severson 1978; Paul Kugler 1979b), and etymological (Lockhart 1978, 1980; Kugelmann), and also grammatical and syntactical experimentation (Ritsema 1976; Hillman 1978a). Other tactical moves concerning emotion, texture, repetitions, reversals, and restatements have been described by Berry (1974).

The primary intention of this verbal work with images is the "recovery of soul in speech" (Sardello 1978a) which at the same time reveals the erotic and aesthetic aspect of images— that they captivate, charm, persuade, and have a rhetorical effect on soul beyond their symbolic content. Image work restores the original poetic sense to images, freeing them from serving a narrational context, having to tell a story with its linear, sequential, and causal implications that foster first-person reports of the egocentric actions and intentions of a personalistic subject. The distinction between image and narrative (Berry 1974; Miller 1976a) is fundamental to the distinction in imaginative style between archetypal polytheistic (q.v.) psychology and traditional psychologies that are egocentered, epic narrations (q.v. therapy).

Three further developments in theory of archetypal images are worth attention. Paul Kugler's work (1978, 1979a) elaborates an acoustic theory of images as structures of invariant meaning apart from linguistic, etymological, semantic, and syntactical meaning. Charles Boer and Peter Kugler (1977) have correlated archetypal images with the theory of perception of J. J. Gibson, asserting that archetypal images are afforded directly by the environment (and are not subjective), so that "archetypal psychology is mythical realism." Casey (1979) sets forth the idea that imagination is so closely related with time, both psychologically and ontologically, that actual image work not only takes time into soul or makes temporal events soul events but also makes time in soul.

4   _Soul_

The primary metaphor of psychology must be soul. Psychology (logos of psyche) etymologically means reason or speech or intelligible account of soul. It is psychology's job to find logos for psyche, to provide soul with an adequate account of itself. Psyche as the *anima mundi*—the Neoplatonic soul of the world—is already there with the world , so that a second task of psychology is to hear psyche speaking through all things of the world, thereby recovering the world as a place of soul (q.v. soul–making).

In its speaking about the soul, archetypal psychology maintains an elusive obliqueness (Romanyshyn 1978–79). This continual carefulness not to substantiate soul follows this maxim: "By soul I mean, first of all, a perspective rather than a substance, a viewpoint toward things rather than a thing itself" (Hillman 1975a, x). In a long examination of "soul," Hillman (1964) concludes: "The soul is a deliberately ambiguous concept resisting all definition in the same manner as do all ultimate symbols which provide the root metaphors for the systems of human thought." In this same passage a circumscription of the term states: "We are not able to use the word in an unambiguous way, even though we take it to refer to that unknown human factor which makes meaning possible, which turns events into experiences, and which is communicated in love." In 1967a, a fourth aspect was added: the soul has a religious concern. And in 1975a (x), three further qualifications were adjoined: "First, 'soul' refers to the *deepening* of events into experiences; second, the significance soul makes possible, whether in love or religious concern, derives from its *special relation with death*. And third, by 'soul' I mean the imaginative possibility in our natures, the experiencing through reflective speculation, dream, image, and *fantasy*—that mode which recognizes all realities as primarily symbolic or metaphorical."

The literalizing and ontologizing dangers attendant upon the elevation of soul to first principle are met by a certain subversive tone in archetypal psychology that speaks of soul events in imagistic, ironic, and even humorous ways (Hillman and Berry 1977). Common to many writers, though different in each—Adolf Guggenbühl–Craig, Miller, Alfred Ziegler, Raphael Lopez–Pedraza, Wolfgang Giegerich, Robert Sardello—is this dark and mordant style. Psyche is kept close to its shadows. There is a continual attempt to break the vessels even as they are being formed.

The term "soul" is also used freely without defining specific usages and senses in order to keep present its connotative power. And it is used interchangeably with the Greek *psyche*, the Greek mythic figure, Psyche (from Apuleius' tale of *Amor and Psyche*), the Germanic *Seele*, and the Latin *anima*. Here "anima" in the more specific Jungian description as a personified figure and function of the imagination (Emma Jung 1957; Hillman 1973c, 1974b) bestows rich imagery, pathologies, and feeling qualities to what otherwise might become only a philosophical concept.

The human being is set within the field of soul; soul is the metaphor that includes the human. "*Dasein as esse in anima* infinitely surpasses man" (Avens 1982a, 185). Even if human life is only one manifestation of the psyche, a human life is always a psychological life—which is how archetypal psychology reads the Aristotelian notion of soul as life and the Christian doctrine of the soul as immortal (i.e. beyond the confines of individual limitation). A humanistic or personalistic psychology will always fail the full perspective of soul that extends beyond human, personal behavior. This move which places humanity within psyche (rather than psyche within humanity) revisions all human activity what-soever as psychological. Every piece of human behavior, whatever its manifest and literal content, is always also a psychological statement.

If every statement has psychological content, then every statement may be scrutinized for its psychological significance, for what it means to soul. Speech about soul—what it is, its body relations, its origins and development, what it consists in, and how it functions—are psychology's concern only because these are the enduring ways the soul gives accounts of itself in conceptual form. They belong to its "*soul–making*" (q.v.), its ongoing fantasy activity, and these accounts called "psychology" ought to be taken fictionally rather than only as positivistic answers about the nature of the soul. The soul can be an object of study only when it is also recognized as the subject studying itself by means of the fictions and metaphors of objectivity. This scrutiny of statements for their psychic implications is a strategical principle of archetypal psychology, providing its tactical method called "psychologizing, or seeing through" (Hillman 1975a, 113-64). The method puts into practice the notion of the unconscious; whatever is stated contains an unconsciousness within the statement. "Unconscious" takes on the meaning of implication and supposition (Berry 1974), that is, what is folded in or held beneath. Statements from any field thus become psychological, or revelations of psyche when their literalism is subverted to allow their suppositions to appear. The strategy implies that psychology cannot be limited to being one field among others since psyche permeates all fields and things.

Anima and Rhetoric

By speaking of soul as a primary metaphor, rather than defining soul substantively and attempting to derive its ontological status from empirical demonstration or theological (metaphysical) argument, archetypal psychology recognizes that psychic reality is inextricably involved with rhetoric. The perspective of soul is inseparable from the manner of speaking of soul, a manner which evokes soul, brings it to life, and persuades us into a psychological perspective. In its concern with rhetoric, archetypal psychology has relied on literary and poetic devices to expound its vision, all the while working at "seeing through" the mechanistic and per-sonalistic metaphors employed by other psychologies so as to recover soul from those literalisms. The polemical foray into others' preserves is necessary to the rhetorical mode.

Soul and Myth

The primary rhetoric of archetypal psychology is myth. Here the path had already been pioneered by Freud, Jung, and Cassirer (Avens 1980), and of course by a tradition of mythical thinking going back through the Romantics and Vico to Plato. This move toward mythical accounts as a psychological language locates psychology in the cultural imagination. Secondly, these myths are themselves metaphors (or, as Vico said "metaphor . . . is a myth [*fabula*] in brief" [S.N. 11, II, 2]), so that by relying on myths as its primary rhetoric, archetypal psychology grounds itself in a fantasy that cannot be taken historically, physically, literally. Even if the recollection of mythology is perhaps the single most characteristic move shared by all "archetypalists," the myths themselves are understood as metaphors—never as transcendental metaphysics whose categories are divine figures. As Hillman (1979a) says: "Myths do not ground, they open." The role of myth in archetypal psychology is not to provide an exhaustive catalogue of possible behaviors or to circumscribe the forms of transpersonal energies (in the Neoplatonic sense) but rather to open the questions of life to transpersonal and culturally imaginative reflection. We may thereby see our ordinary lives embedded in and ennobled by the dramatic and world-creative life of mythical figures (Bedford 1981). The study of mythology allows events to be recognized against their mythical background. More important, however, is that the study of mythology enables one to perceive and experience the life of the soul mythically.

5   *Soul, Metaphor and Fantasy*

The philosophical problem "how to define soul" or how to state a "logos of soul" (Christou 1963) must be viewed in the first place as a psychological phenomenon, one that arises from the soul's own desire for self-knowledge which can best be satisfied in terms of its own constitution: images. Thus the logos of soul (i.e. a true speaking of it), will be in an imagistic style, an account or "*recit*" (Corbin 1979, 43f.) that is metaphorical.

The statement above that "the primary metaphor of psychology must be soul" attempts two things: (a) to state the soul's nature in its own language (metaphor) and (b) to recognize that all statements in psychology about soul are metaphors. In this way, soul-as-metaphor leads beyond the problem of "how to define soul" and encourages an account of the soul toward imagining itself rather than defining itself. Here metaphor serves a psychological function; it becomes an instrument of soul–making (q.v.) rather than a mere "figure of speech," because it transposes the soul's questioning about its nature to a mythopoesis of actual imagining, an ongoing psychological creation (Berry 1982).

Soul–as–metaphor also describes how the soul acts. It performs as does a metaphor, transposing meaning and releasing interior, buried significance. Whatever is heard with the ear of soul reverberates with under– and overtones (Moore 1978). The perspective darkens with a deeper light. But this metaphorical perspective also kills; it brings about the death of naive realism, naturalism, and literal understanding. The relation of soul to death—a theme running all through archetypal psychology—is thus a function of the psyche's metaphorical activity. The metaphorical mode does not speak in declarative statements or explain in clear contrasts. It delivers all things to their shadows. So its perspective defeats heroic attempts to gain a grip on phenomena. Instead the metaphorical mode of soul is "elusive, allusive, illusive" (Romanyshyn 1977), undermining the definition of consciousness as intentionality and its history as development.

Human awareness fails in its comprehension not because of original sin or personal neurosis or because of the obstinacy of the objective world to which it is supposedly opposed. Human awareness fails, according to a psychology based on soul, because the soul's metaphorical nature has a suicidal

necessity (Hillman 1964), an underworld affiliation (Hillman
1979a), a "morbism" (Ziegler 1980), a destiny—different
from dayworld claims—which makes the psyche fundamentally unable to submit to the *hubris* of an egocentric notion
of subjectivity as achievement (*Leistung*), defined as cog-
nition, conation, intention, perception, and so forth.

Thus that sense of weakness (Lopez–Pedraza 1977,
1982), inferiority (Hillman 1977c), mortification (Berry
1973), masochism (Cowan 1979), darkness (Winquist 1981),
and failure (Hillman 1972b) is inherent to the *mode* of metaphor which defeats conscious understanding as a control over
phenomena. Metaphor, as the soul's *mode* of logos, ultimately
results in that abandonment to the given which approximates
mysticism (Avens 1980).

The metaphorical transposition—this "death-dealing"
move that at the same time re-awakens consciousness to a
sense of soul—is at the heart of archetypal psychology's
mission, its world intention. As Freud and Jung both attempted
to discover the fundamental "mistake" in Western culture
so as to resolve the misery of man trapped in the decline of
the West, so archetypal psychology specifies this mistake
as loss of soul which it further identifies with loss of images
and the imaginal sense. The result has been an intensification
of subjectivity (Durand 1975), showing both in the self-enclosed
egocentricity and the hyperactivism, or life-fanaticism, of
Western (rather, Northern q.v.) consciousness which has lost
its relation with death and the underworld.

That re-imagining and re-animating of the cultural
psyche to which archetypal psychology aspires necessitates
pathologizing (q.v.), for only this weakening or "falling apart"
(Hillman 1975a) breaks through self-enclosed subjectivity and

restores it to its depth in soul, allowing soul to reappear again in the world of things.

The re-animation of things by means of metaphor was already indicated by Vico (S.N. II, I, 2) who wrote that "metaphor . . . gives sense and passion to insensate things." As the metaphorical perspective gives new animation to soul, so too it re–vitalizes areas that had been assumed not ensouled and not psychological: the events of the body and medicine, the ecological world, the man-made phenomena of architecture and transportation, education, food, bureaucratic language and systems. These have all been examined as metaphorical images and have become subject to intense psychological revision by Sardello and his students first at the University of Dallas and at The Dallas Institute of Humanities and Culture. The metaphorical perspective which revisions worldly phenomena as images can find "sense and passion" where the Cartesian mind sees the mere extension of de-souled insensate objects. In this way, the poetic basis of mind (q.v.) takes psychology out of the confines of laboratory and consulting room, and even beyond the personal subjectivity of the human person, into a psychology of things as objectifications of images with interiority, things as the display of fantasy.

For archetypal psychology, "fantasy" and "reality" change places and values. First, they are no longer opposed. Second, fantasy is never merely mentally subjective but is always being enacted and embodied (Hillman 1972a, xxxix-xl). Third, whatever is physically or literally 'real' is always also a fantasy image. Thus the world of so-called hard factual reality is always also the display of a specifically shaped fantasy, as if to say, along with Wallace Stevens, the American philosopher-poet of imagination on whom archetypal psychology often draws, there is always "a poem at the heart of things." Jung stated the same idea (*CW* 6, §18): "The psyche creates reality everyday. The only expression I can say for this activity is fantasy." And he takes the word "fantasy" "from poetic usage" (*CW* 6, §743).

The latest explorations of archetypal psychology—some published in the *Spring Journal* 1979-97—have been in the direction of poetics, aesthetics, and literary criticism. This is less the influence of contemporary psychoanalytic concerns with language than it is the re-appraisal of psychology itself as an activity of poesis and the fact that fantasy is the archetypal activity of the psyche.

6 Soul and Spirit

If imagining is the native activity of the *anima mundi*, then fantasy is always going on and is not subject to a phenomenological *epoché* (Husserl: setting aside or bracketing out in order to move directly to the event itself). Moreover, if fantasy is always going on, then *epoché* is itself a fantasy: of isolating, of objectification, and of a consciousness that can be truly addressed by phenomena as they are. Archetypal psychology maintains, however, that we can never be purely phenomenal or truly objective. One is never beyond the subjectivism given with the soul's native dominants of fantasy structures. These dominate subjective perspectives and organize them into "stances," so that the only objectivity that could be approximated results from the subjective eye turned

in on itself, regarding its own regard, examining its own perspective for the archetypal subjects (q.v. personifying) who are
at this moment governing our way of being in the world among
phenomena. Psychology as an objective science is forever im-
possible once one has recognized that objectivity is itself a poetic
genre (similar to "writer-as-mirror" in French naturalism), a
mode that constructs the world so that things appear as sheer
things (not faces, not animated, not with interiority), subject to
will, separate from each other, mute, without sense or passion.

One position is particularly obdurate in yielding to
the fantasy that fantasy is always going on, and that is the
stance of spirit. It appears as scientific objectivity, as metaphysics, and as theology. And where archetypal psychology
has attacked these approaches, it is part of a wider strategy
to distinguish the methods and rhetoric of soul from those
of spirit, so that soul is not forced to forfeit its style to fulfill
the obligations required by a spiritual perspective, whether
philosophical, scientific, or religious. For psychology to be
possible at all it must keep the distinction between soul and
spirit (Hillman 1976; 1975a, 67-70; 1977a).

At times the spirit position with its rhetoric of order,
number, knowledge, permanency, and self-defensive logic has
been discussed as "senex" and Saturnian (Vitale 1973; Hillman
1975d); at other times, because of its rhetoric of clarity and
detached observation, it has been discussed as Apollonic
(Hillman 1972c); on other occasions, because of the rhetoric
of unity, ultimacy, identity, it has been termed "monotheistic;"
and in yet other contexts, "heroic" and also "puer" (1967b).

While recognizing that the spirit perspective must
place itself above (as the soul places itself as inferior) and
speak in transcendent, ultimate, and pure terms, archetypal

psychology conceives its task to be one of imagining the spirit language of "truth," "faith," "law," and the like as a rhetoric of spirit, even if spirit is obliged by this same rhetoric to take its stance truthfully and faithfully, i.e., literally.

The distinction between soul and spirit further guards against psychological therapy becoming confused with spiritual disciplines—whether Eastern or Western—and gives yet another reason for archetypal psychology to eschew borrowings from meditative techniques and/or operant conditioning, both of which conceptualize psychic events in spiritual terms.

7 Soul–Making

The underlying aspiration of its work, archetypal psychology has called "soul–making," taking the phrase from the poets William Blake and, particularly, John Keats: "Call the world if you please, 'The vale of Soul–making.' Then you will find out the use of the world . . ." For all its emphasis upon the individualized soul, archetypal psychology sets this soul, and its making, squarely in the midst of the world. And, it does not seek a way out of or beyond the world toward redemption or mystical transcendence, because "The way through the world is more difficult to find than the way beyond it" (Wallace Stevens, "Reply to Papini"). The curative or salvational vision of archetypal psychology focuses upon the soul in the world which is also the soul of the world (*anima mundi*). The idea of soul–making by taking any world event as also a place of soul insists that even this

Neoplatonic and "arcane" psychology is nonetheless embedded in the "vale" and its engagement therein. The
artificial tension between soul and world, private and public, interior and exterior thus disappears when the soul as
anima mundi, and its making, is located in the world.

More specifically, the act of soul–making is imagining,
since images are the psyche, its stuff, and its perspective.
Crafting images-such as discussed below in regard to therapy
(q.v.)—is thus an equivalent of soul–making. This crafting
can take place in the concrete modes of the artisan, a work
of the hands, and with the morality of the hands. And, it can
take place in sophisticated elaborations of reflection, religion,
relationships, social action, so long as these activities are imagined from the perspective of soul, soul as uppermost concern.

In other words, only when imagination is recognized
as an engagement at the borders of the human and a work in
relation with mythic dominants can this articulation of images be considered a psycho–poesis (Miller 1976b) or
soul–making. Its intention is the realization of the images—
for they are the psyche—and not merely of the human
subject. As Corbin has said: "It is their individuation, not
ours," suggesting that soul–making can be most succinctly
defined as the individuation of imaginal reality.

Soul–making is also described as imaging, that is,
seeing or hearing by means of an imagining which sees
through an event to its image. Imaging means releasing
events from their literal understanding into a mythical appreciation. *Soul–making*, in this sense, is equated with
de-literalizing—that psychological attitude which suspiciously
disallows the naive and given level of events in order to
search out their shadowy, metaphorical significances for soul.

So the question of soul–making is "what does this event, this thing, this moment move in my soul? What does it mean to my death?" The question of death enters because it is in regard to death that the perspective of soul is distinguished most starkly from the perspective of natural life.

Soul–making does imply a metaphysical fantasy, and the implied metaphysics of archetypal psychology are best found in *The Dream and the Underworld* (Hillman 1979a) which elaborates the relations between psyche and death. There the dream is taken as the paradigm of the psyche—where the psyche presents itself encompassing the ego and engaged in its own work (dream-work). From the dream, one may assume that the psyche is fundamentally concerned with its imaginings and only secondarily concerned with subjective experiences in the dayworld which the dream transforms into images, i.e., into soul. The dream is thus making soul each night. Images become the means of translating life–events into soul, and this work, aided by the conscious elaboration of imagination, builds an imaginal vessel, or "ship of death" (a phrase taken from D. H. Lawrence), that is similar to the subtle body, or *ochema* of the Neoplatonists (cf. Avens 1982b). The question of the soul's immortality is not directly answered by a metaphysical statement. Rather, the very nature of the soul in the dream—or at least the perspective of soul toward the dream—shows its inattention to and disregard for mortal experience as such, even for physical death itself, receiving into its purview only those faces and events from the mortal world that bear upon the opus of its destiny.

8   Depth and the Vertical Direction

Since its beginning in Freud's study of the deep layers of
the mind—prey sub-, or un-conscious—the field of "depth
psychology" (so named at the turn of the century by the
Zürich psychiatrist Eugen Bleuler) has always been directed
downward, whether toward buried memories of childhood
or toward archaic mythologems. Archetypal psychology has
taken this depth metaphor equally seriously—though less
literally. It has carried the metaphor of depth of soul back in
history to Heraclitus (Diels–Kranz, Frag. 45: *bathun*) and
then to Augustine's *thesaurus* or *memoria (Confessions X)*.
Moreover, it has reverted Freud's own move into depth, the
descent into the dream as described in his *Traumdeutung*, to
the mythologies of the Underworld, Hades, Persephone,
Dionysus—and to Christian theologies of descent (Miller
1981b)—exploring the fundamental relation of the psyche
with the realm of the dead which is also the realm of images
or *eidola* (Hillman 1979a).

　　　Because of the vertical direction of depth psychology,
it is obliged to be concerned with depression and with the
reduction of phenomena to their "deadly" essence, their
pathologized (q.v.) extremity (Berry 1973), where we experience them as both materially destructive and negative and
yet as the ground of support (Berry 1978b).

　　　The literalization of downwardness in depth psychology has resulted in a narrowness of meaning: introverted
inwardness within the person, into the "abyss" and "secret
chamber" of the personal self (Augustine). What then of
the relationship with others, with the horizontal world?

For archetypal psychology, the vertical direction refers to interiority as a capacity within all things. All things have an archetypal significance and are available to psychological penetration, and this interiority is manifested by the physiognomic character of the things of the horizontal world. Depth is therefore not literally hidden, deep down, inside. Rather, the fantasy of depth encourages us to look at the world again, to read each event for "something deeper," to "insearch" (Hillman 1967a), rather than to research, for yet further significance below what seems merely evident and natural. The downward interiorizing fantasy is thus at the basis of all psychoanalysis. The fantasy of hidden depths ensouls the world and fosters imagining ever deeper into things. Depth—rather than a literal or physical location—is a primary metaphor necessary for psychological thinking (or "psychologizing," Hillman 1975a).

9 *Cultural Locus: North and South*

The downward direction may also be envisioned as Southward. Unlike the main psychologies of the twentieth century which have drawn their sources from Northern Europe—the German language and the Protestant–Jewish monotheistic *Weltanschauung*—archetypal psychology starts in the South. Neither Greek nor Renaissance civilization developed "psychologies" as such. The word "psychology" and most modern psychological terms (Hillman 1972c) do not appear in an active sense until the nineteenth century. In recognition of these historical facts, archetypal psychology situates its work in a pre-psychological geography, where the culture of imagination and the modes of living carried what had to be formulated in the North as "psychology." "Psychology" is a necessity of a post-reformational culture that had been deprived of its poetic base.

Since, as Casey (1982) maintains, place is prior to the possibility of thought—all thought must be placed in order to be—archetypal psychology requires an imaginal location. Freud's "Vienna" and Jung's "Zürich," or the "California Schools" are fantasy locations, not merely sociological and historical contexts. They place the ideas in a geographical image. Such is "south" in the imagination of archetypal psychology.

"South" is both an ethnic, cultural, geographic place and a symbolic one. It is both the Mediterranean culture, its images and textual sources, its sensual and concrete humanity, its Gods and Goddesses and their myths, its tragic and picaresque genres (rather than the epic heroism of the North); and it is a symbolic stance "below the border" which does not view that region of the soul only from a northern moralistic perspective. The unconscious thus becomes radically re–visioned and may as well be located "up north" (as Aryan, Apollonic, Germanic, positivistic, voluntaristic, rationalistic, Cartesian, Protestant, scientistic, personalistic, monotheistic, etc.). Even the family, rather than a source of "northern" neurosis, can be revalued as the ground of ancestral and societal binding.

By remembering this fundamental division in Western cultural history, archetypal psychology eludes the conventional dilemma of "East and West." Positions usually given over to the "East" are included within archetypal psychology's own orientation. Having re-oriented consciousness toward non-ego factors—the multiple personifications of the soul, the elaboration of the imaginal ground of myths, the direct immediacy of sense experience coupled with the ambiguity of its interpretation, and the radically relative phenomenality of the "ego" itself as but one fantasy of the psyche—archetypal psychology makes superfluous the move toward oriental disciplines which have had to be found in the East when psychology is identified with the perspectives of northern psychic geography.

Roberts Avens's monographs (1980, 1982a, b) show that archetypal psychology is nothing less than a parallel formulation of certain Eastern philosophies. Like them, it too dissolves ego, ontology, substantiality, literalisms of self and divisions between it and things—the entire conceptual apparatus which northern psychology constructs from the heroic ego and in its defense—into the psychic reality of imagination experienced in immediacy. The "emptying out" of Western positivism comparable to a Zen exercise or a way of Nirvana, is precisely what archetypal psychology has effectuated, though by means that are utterly Western, where "Western" refers to a psychology of soul as imagined in the tradition of the South.

10 Polytheistic Psychology and Religion

Of all the moves, none is so far-reaching in cultural implication as the attempt to recover the perspectives of polytheism. Moore (1980) considers this perspective to be the rational consequent of a psychology based in anima which can "animate" the study of religion by offering both "a way of understanding religion . . . and a way of going about religious studies" (284). Miller's christology (1981a) demonstrates the relevance of the polytheistic perspective for even a religion whose dogma historically derives from an anti-polytheistic position. The complex issues of the new polytheism have been treated by Miller (1974, with an appendix by Hillman 1981) and by Goldenberg (1979). The polytheistic moves of archetypal psychology occur in four interrelated modes.

(1) The most accurate model of human existence will be able to account for its innate diversity, both among individuals and within each individual. Yet, this same model must also provide fundamental structures and values for this diversity. For both Freud and Jung, multiplicity is basic to human nature, and their models of man rely upon a polycentric fantasy. Freud's notion of the child as sexually polymorphous originates the libido in a polymorphic, polyvalent, and polycentric field of erogenous zones. Jung's model of personality (q.v.) is essentially multiple, and Jung correlates the plurality of its archetypal structure with the polytheistic stage of culture (*CW* 9, ii, §427). Hence, "the soul's inherent multiplicity demands a theological fantasy of equal differentiation" (Hillman 1975a, 167).

(2) The tradition of thought (Greek, Renaissance, Romantic) to which archetypal psychology claims it is an heir is set in polytheistic attitudes. The imaginative products of these historical periods cannot contribute further to psychology unless the consciousness that would receive from them is able to transpose itself into a similar polytheistic framework. The high achievements of Western culture from which contemporary culture may find sources for its survival remain

closed to modern consciousness unless it gains a perspective mimetic to what it is examining. Hence, polytheistic psychology is necessary for the continuity of culture.

(3) The social, political, and psychiatric critique implied throughout archetypal psychology mainly concerns the monotheistic hero-myth (now called ego-psychology) of secular humanism, i.e., the single-centered, self-identified notion of subjective consciousness of humanism (from Protagoras to Sartre). It is this myth which has dominated the soul and which leads to unreflected action and self-blindness (Oedipus). It is responsible also for the repression of a psychological diversity that then appears as psychopathology. Hence, a polytheistic psychology is necessary for reawakening reflective consciousness and bringing a new reflection to psychopathology.

(4) The *perspectivalism* of archetypal psychology requires a deepening of subjectivity beyond mere Nietzschean perspectives or existential stances. Perspectives are *forms* of vision, rhetoric, values, epistemology, and lived styles that perdure independently of empirical individuality. For archetypal psychology, pluralism and multiplicity and relativism are not enough: these are merely philosophical generalities. Psychology needs to specify and differentiate each event, which it can do against the variegated background of archetypal configurations, or what polytheism called Gods, in order to make multiplicity both authentic and precise. Thus the question it asks of an event is not *why* or *how*, but rather *what* specifically is being presented and ultimately *who*, which divine figure, is speaking in this style of consciousness, this form of presentation. Hence, a polytheistic psychology is necessary for the authorization of "a

pluralistic universe" (William James 1909), for consistencies within it, and for precision of its differentiation.

The polytheistic analogy is both religious and not religious (Miller 1972, 1974; Bregman 1980; Scott 1980; Avens 1980). The Gods are taken essentially, as foundations, so that psychology points beyond soul and can never be merely agnostic. The sacred and sacrificial dimension—the religious instinct as Jung calls it—is given a place of main value; and, in truth, it is precisely because of the appeal to the Gods that value enters the psychological field, creating claims on each human life and giving personal acts more than personal significance. The Gods are therefore the Gods of religion and not mere nomina, categories, devices *ex machina*. They are respected as powers and persons and creators of value.

A distinction is nonetheless maintained between polytheism as psychology and as religion. This distinction is difficult because "depth analysis leads to the soul which inevitably involves analysis in religion and even in theology, while at the same time living religion, experienced religion, originates in the human psyche and is as such a psychological phenomenon" (Hillman 1967a, 42). When soul is the first metaphor (q.v.), then psychology and religion must be intertwined and their distinction arbitrary or ambiguous. The question of polytheism is posed by the soul itself as soon as its perspective experiences the world as animated and its own nature as replete with changing diversity. That is, as soon as the soul is freed from ego domination, the question of polytheism arises.

Yet archetypal psychology is "not out to worship Greek Gods or those of any other polytheistic high culture . . . We are not reviving a dead faith. For we are not concerned

[handwritten margin notes: "for metaphor for modes of experience", "← Patience", "imagined thru personifying, pathologizing, psychologizing"]

with faith" (Hillman 1975a, 170; cf. A. H. Armstrong 1981). The Gods of psychology are not believed in, not taken literally, not imagined theologically. "Religion approaches Gods with ritual, prayer, sacrifice, worship, creed . . . . In archetypal psychology, Gods are _imagined_. They are approached through psychological methods of personifying, pathologizing, and psychologizing. They are formulated ambiguously, as metaphors for modes of experience and as numinous borderline persons. They are cosmic perspectives in which the soul participates" (ibid., 169). Mainly, the mode of this participation is reflection: the Gods are discovered in recognizing the stance of one's perspective, one's psychological sensitivity to the configurations that dominate one's styles of thought and life. Gods for psychology do not have to be experienced in direct mystical encounter or in effigies, whether as concrete figures or as theological definitions.

A saying attributed to Hegel declares: "what is required is a 'monotheism of reason and heart, a polytheism of imagination and art'" (Cook 1973). Inasmuch as archetypal psychology is imaginative, it requires imaginative first principles and polytheism becomes necessary, although it definitely does not carry on the rationalist separation between heart and art, between valuative and aesthetic sensitivities.

The critique of theological religion continues that done by Freud and Jung, though with an even more radical cast. Archetypal psychology does not attempt to correct the Judeo Christian religion as illusion (Freud) or transform it as onesided (Jung). It shifts the ground of the entire question to a polytheistic position. In this single stroke, it carries out Freud's and Jung's critiques to their ultimate consequent— the death of God as a monotheistic fantasy, while at the same time restoring the fullness of the Gods in all things and, let it be said, reverting psychology itself to the recognition that it too is a religious activity (Hillman 1975a, 227). If a religious instinct is inherent to the psyche as Jung maintained, then any psychology attempting to do justice to the psyche must recognize its religious nature.

A polytheistic vision differs from undifferentiated pantheism, holy vitalism, and naturalistic animism—which from the standpoint of monotheistic consciousness tend to be bunched together as "pagan" and "primitive." Gods in archetypal psychology are not some primal energy suffused through the universe nor are they imagined to be independent magical powers working on us through things. Gods are imagined as the formal intelligibility of the phenomenal world, allowing each thing to be discerned for its inherent intelligibility and for its specific place of belonging to this or that kosmos (ordered pattern or arrangement). The Gods are places, and myths make place for psychic events that in an only human world become pathological. By offering shelter and altar, the Gods can order and make intelligible the entire phenomenal world of nature and human consciousness. All phenomena are "saved" by the act of placing them which at once gives them value. We discover what belongs where by means of likeness, the analogy of events with mythical configurations. This mode was current during millennia of our culture in alchemy, planetary astrology, natural philosophy, and medicine, each of which studied the microcosmic things in rapport with macrocosmic Gods (Moore 1982; Boer 1980). It was this question of *placing* that was addressed to the Greek oracles: "To what gods or hero must I pray or sacrifice to achieve such and such a purpose?" If one knows where an event belongs, to whom it can be related, then one is able to proceed.

Today, however, the discovery of what belongs where, the *epistrophé* or reversion through likeness of an event to its mythical pattern, is less the aim of archetypal psychology than is an archetypal sensitivity that all things belong to myth. The study of these archetypal placings, deriving from the work of Frances Yates (1966) in regard to the Memory Theatre of the Florentine, Giulio Camillo (c. 1480–1544), has been carried out in some detail in seminars by Raphael Lopez–Pedraza and by Robert Sardello.

11   *Psychopathology*

The point of departure for the re-visioning of psychopathology is a statement from Jung (1929, *CW* 13, §54): "The gods have become diseases; Zeus no longer rules Olympus but rather the solar plexus, and produces curious specimens for the doctor's consulting room . . . ."

The link between Gods and diseases is double: on the one hand, giving the dignity of archetypal significance and divine reflection to every symptom whatsoever, and on the other hand, suggesting that myth and its figures may be examined for patterns of pathology. Hillman (1974a) has called this pathology in mythical figures the *infirmitas* of the archetype, by which is meant both the essential "infirmity" of all archetypal forms—that they are not perfect, not transcendent, not idealizations—and that they therefore provide "nursing" to human conditions; they are the embracing backgrounds within which our personal sufferings can find support and be cared for.

The double link—that pathology is mythologized and mythology is pathologized—had already been adumbrated by Freud's presentation of the Oedipus myth as the key to the pathology of neurosis and even of the civilization as a whole. Before Freud, the link between *mythos* and *pathos* can be discovered in Nietzsche's *Birth of Tragedy* and in the scholarly research of the great German classicist and encyclopaedist, Wilhelm Heinrich Roscher, whose *Ephialtes* (1900), a monograph on Pan and the Nightmare, was subtitled "A Mythopathological Study" (cf. Hillman 1972a).

The relations between myths and psychopathology are elaborated in a series of studies: Raphael Lopez–Pedraza (1977) on Hermes and (1982) on the Titans; Patricia Berry (1975) on Demeter/Persephone and (1979b) on Echo; Thomas Moore (1979a) on Artemis; Neil Micklem (1979) on Medusa; Hillman (1970a, 1975d) on Saturn, (1974a) on Athene and Ananke, (1972c) on Eros and on Dionysus, (1972a) on Pan, and (1967b) on the puer eternus or divinely youthful figure in various mythologies; Murray Stein (1973) on Hephaistos and (1977) on Hera. In these studies, the myth is examined for its pathological implications. The hermeneutic begins with myths and mythical figures (not with a case), reading them downward for psychological understanding of the fantasies going on in behavior.

Thereby archetypal psychology follows the epistrophic (reversion) method of Corbin, returning to the higher principle in order to find place for and understand the lesser—the images before their examples. Imagination becomes a method for investigating and comprehending psychopathology. This hermeneutic method is also essentially Neoplatonic; it is the preferred way for deciphering the grotesque and pathologized configurations of Renaissance psychology. As Wind says in his "Observation on Method" (1967, 238): "The common-place may be understood as a reduction of the exceptional, but the exceptional cannot be understood by amplifying the commonplace. Both logically and causally the exceptional is crucial, because it introduces . . . the more comprehensive category."

Precisely because myth presents the exceptional, the outlandish, and more-than-human dimension, it offers background to the sufferings of souls *in extremis*, i.e., what nineteenth–century medicine calls "psychopathology." The double movement between pathology and mythology moreover implies that the pathological is always going on in human life inasmuch as life enacts mythical fantasies. Archetypal psychology further claims that it is mainly through the wounds in human life that the Gods enter (rather than through pronouncedly sacred or mystical events), because pathology is the most palpable manner of bearing witness to the powers beyond ego control and the insufficiency of the ego perspective.

This perpetually recurring "pathologizing" is defined as "the psyche's autonomous ability to create illness, morbidity, disorder, abnormality, and suffering in any aspect of its behavior and to experience and imagine life through this deformed and afflicted perspective" (Hillman 1975a, 57). There is no cure of pathologizing; there is, instead, a re-evaluation.

That pathologizing is also a "deformed perspective" accounts for its place in the work of imagination which, according to Gaston Bachelard (1884–1962)—another major source of the archetypal tradition—must proceed by "deforming the images offered by perception" (Bachelard 1943, 7). It is this pathologized eye which, like that of the artist and the psychoanalyst, prevents the phenomena of the soul from being naively understood as merely natural. Following Jung (and his research into alchemy), psychological work is an *opus contra naturam.* This idea Hillman (1975a, 84-96) follows further by attacking the "naturalistic fallacy" which dominates most normative psychologies.

Another direction of the *mythos/pathos* connection starts with one specific form of pathology, searching it for its mythical possibilities, as if to uncover "the God in the disease." Examples are: Lockhart (1977) cancer; Moore (1979b) asthma; Leveranz (1979) epilepsy; Hawkins (1979) migraine; Severson (1979) skin disorders; Kugelmann, glaucoma; Sipiora (1981) tuberculosis.

There are also more general reflections upon pathology revisioned within an archetypal hermeneutic: Robert Stein (1974) on psychosexual disorders; Guggenbühl–Craig (1971) on the archetypal power problem in medical attitudes; Ziegler (1980) on archetypal medicine; Sardello (1980a) on medicine, disease, and the body. These works look at the body, pathology, and its treatment altogether free from the positivism of the clinical and empirical traditions that have come down to the twentieth century from nineteenth-century scientistic, materialistic medicine, its views of health, disease, and the power-hero role of the physician.

In one respect, the position here is close to the antipsychiatry of Thomas Szasz and R. D. Laing. Each regards "abnormal" conditions as existentially human and hence fundamentally normal. They become psychiatric conditions when looked at psychiatrically. Archetypal psychology, however, makes three further moves beyond anti-psychiatry. First, it examines the normalizing perspective itself in order to show its "abnormalities" and pathologizing propensities. Second, unlike Szasz and Laing, archetypal psychology maintains the real existence of psychopathology as such, as inherent to psychic reality. It neither denies psychopathology nor attempts to find cause for it outside the soul in politics, professional power, or social convention. Third, because pathologizing is inherent to psyche, it is also necessary. The necessity of pathologizing derives, on the one hand, from the Gods who show patterns of psychopathology and, on the other hand, from the soul which becomes aware of its destiny in death mainly through the psyche's indefatigable and amazingly inventive capacity to pathologize.

As Freud's paradigm of psychopathology was hysteria (and paranoia) and Jung's was schizophrenia, archetypal psychology has so far spoken mainly about depression (Hillman 1972c, 1975a, c, d, 1979a; Vitale 1973; Berry 1975, 1978b; Guggenbühl–Craig 1979; Miller 1981b; Simmer 1981) and mood disorder (Sardello 1980b). Depression has also provided a focus for *Kulturkritik*, an attack upon social and medical conventions that do not allow the vertical depth of depressions.

For, a society that does not allow its individuals "to go down" cannot find its depth and must remain permanently inflated in a manic mood disorder disguised as "growth." Hillman (1975a, 98) links the Western horror of depression with the tradition of the heroic ego and Christian salvation through upward resurrection. "Depression is still the Great Enemy . . . Yet through depression we enter depths and in depths find soul. Depression is essential to the tragic sense of life. It moistens the dry soul and dries the wet. It brings refuge, limitation, focus, gravity, weight, and humble power-lessness. It reminds of death. The true revolution (in behalf of soul) begins in the individual who can be true to his or her depression."

12   *The Practice of Therapy*

Archetypal psychology continues the ritual procedures of classical analysis deriving from Freud and Jung: (1) regular meetings (2) with individual patients (3) face-to-face (4) at the therapist's locus (5) for a fee. (Groups, couples, and children are generally eschewed; minor attention is paid to diagnostic and typological categories and to psychological testing.) These five procedures, however, are not rigid, and any of them may be modified or abandoned. Classical analysis (Hillman 1975b, 101) has been defined as: "a course of treatment in an atmosphere of sympathy and confidence of one person by another person for a fee, which treatment may be conceived as educative in various senses or therapeutic in various senses and which proceeds principally through the joint interpretative exploration of habitual behavior and of classes of mental events that have been traditionally called fantasies, feelings, memories, dreams and ideas, and where the exploration follows a coherent set of methods, concepts and beliefs stemming mainly from Freud and from Jung, where focus is preferably upon the unanticipated and affectively charged, and whose goal is the improvement (subjectively and/or objectively determined) of the analysand and the termination of the treatment."

If analysis "terminates," then it is governed by linear time. Casey (1979, 157) exposes this assumption: ". . . the time of soul is not to be presumed continuous . . . it is discontinuous, not simply as having breaks or gaps . . . but as having many avatars, many kinds and modes. The polycentricity of the psyche demands no less than this, namely, a polyform time . . . ." That analyses have been growing longer since the early years with Freud and Jung must be understood as a phenomenon of the soul's temporality: "It is the soul, after all, that is taking all this extra time, and it must be doing so for reasons of its own which have primarily to do with . . . taking more world-time so as to encourage the efflorescence of its own imaginal time" (ibid., 156).

Practice is rooted in Jung's view of the psyche as inherently purposeful: all psychic events whatsoever have *telos*. Archetypal psychology, however, does not enunciate this telos. Purposefulness qualifies psychic events, but it is not to be literalized apart from the images in which it inheres. Thus archetypal psychology refrains from stating goals for therapy (individuation or wholeness) and for its phenomena such as symptoms and dreams (compensations, warnings, prophetic indications). Purpose remains a *perspective* toward events in Jung's original description of the prospective versus the reductive view. Positive formulations of the telos of analysis lead only into teleology and dogmas of goals. Archetypal psychology fosters the sense of purpose as therapeutic in itself because it enhances the patient's interest in psychic phenomena, including the most objectionable symptoms, as intentional. But the therapist does not literalize these intentions, and therefore therapy follows the Freudian mode of restraint and abstention. It moves along a *via negativa*, attempting to deliteralize all formulations of purpose so that the analysis is reduced to sticking with the actual images.

The specific focus and atmosphere of archetypal psychology's way of working and further departures from classical analysis must be culled from many publications for two reasons: there is no program of training (no didactic), and no single work lays out the theory of the practice of therapy. (Publications particularly relevant are: Guggenbühl–Craig 1970, 1971, 1972, 1979; Berry 1978a, 1981; Hillman and Berry 1977; Grinned 1973; Frey, Bosnak et al. 1978; Giegerich 1977; Hillman 1975a, 1972a, 1964, 1977b, c, 1975c, 1974a; Hartman 1980; Newman 1980; Watkins 1981.)

Departures from classical analysis lie less in the form of therapy than in its focus. Archetypal psychology conceives therapy, as it does psychopathology, as the enactment of fantasy. Rather than prescribe or employ therapy for pathology, it self-examines the fantasy of therapy (so that therapy does not perpetuate the literal pathology which calls therapy forth and is called forth by a literal therapy). Archetypal psychology seeks to remind therapy of its notions of itself (Giegerich 1977), attempting to lift repression from the unconsciousness of therapy itself.

In "The Fiction of Case History," Hillman (1975c) examines the case model used by Freud, and by analysts ever since, as a style of narrative. At once, the problem of cases and the problems told by cases become the subject of an imaginative, literary reflection of which the clinical is only one genre. Genres or categories of the literary imagination —epic, detective, comic, social realist, picaresque—become relevant for understanding the organization of narratives told in therapy. Since "the way we tell our story is the way we form our therapy" (Berry 1974, 69), the entire procedure of therapeutic work must be reconceived in terms of the poetic basis of mind. An essential work of therapy is to become conscious of the fictions in which the patient is cast and to re-write or ghost-write, collaboratively, the story by re-telling it in a more profound and authentic style. In this re-told version in which imaginative art becomes the model, the personal failures and sufferings of the patient are essential to the story as they are to art.

The *explication du text* (with which the examination in therapy of images and narrative details can be compared) derives in part from the "personal construct theory" (1955) of George Kelly (1905-1966). Experience is never raw or brute; it is always constructed by images which are revealed in the patient's narrations. The fantasy in which a problem is set tells more about the way the problem is constructed and how it can be transformed (reconstructed) than does any attempt at analyzing the problem in its own terms.

A paper presented by Hillman and Berry at the First International Seminar of Archetypal Psychology January 1977) declares: "Ours could be called *an image-focused therapy.* Thus the dream as an image or bundle of images is paradigmatic, as if we were placing the entire psychotherapeutic procedure within the context of a dream" (cf. Berry 1974, 1978a, and Hillman 1977b, 1978a, 1979a, b, for method and examples of dream work). It is not, however, that dreams as such become the focus of therapy but that all events are regarded from a dream-viewpoint, as if they were images, metaphorical expressions. The dream is not in the patient and something he or she does or makes; the patient is in the dream and is doing or being made by its fiction. These same papers on dream work exhibit how an image can be created, that is, how an event can be heard as metaphor through various manipulations: grammatical reversals, removal of punctuation, restatement and echo, humor, amplification. The aim of working with dreams or life events as dreams is to bring reflection to declarative and unreflected discourse, so that words no longer believe they refer to objective referents; instead, speech becomes imagistic, self-referent, descriptive of a psychic condition as its very expression (Berry 1982).

The detailed examination of presentational images— whether from dreams, from life situations, or the waking imagination of fantasy—has been a subject for Watkins (1976); Garufi (1977); Humbert (1971); Berry (1979a, b); Hillman (1977a, c). Here the work is a further refinement of Jung's technique of "active imagination" (Hull 1971).

Active imagination at times becomes the method of choice in therapy. There is direct perception of and engagement with an imaginary figure or figures. These figures with whom one converses or performs actions or which one depicts plastically are not conceived to be merely internal projections or only parts of the personality (q.v.). They are given the respect and dignity due independent beings. They are imagined seriously, though *not literally*. Rather like Neoplatonic daimones, and like angels in Corbin's sense, their "between" reality is neither physical nor metaphysical, although just "as real as you—as a psychic entity—are real" (Jung, *CW* 14, §753). This development of true imaginative power (the *vera imaginatio* of Paracelsus; the *himma* of the heart of Corbin) and the ability to live one's life in the company of ghosts, familiars, ancestors, guides—the populace of the metaxy—are also aims of an archetypal therapy (Hillman 1977c, 1979c).

Recently, image–focused therapy has extended into the sensate world of perceptual objects and habitual forms— buildings, bureaucratic systems, conventional language, transportation, urban environment, food, education. This project has no less an ambition than the recuperation of the *anima mundi* or soul of the world by scrutinizing the face of the world as aesthetic physiognomy. This move envisages therapy altogether beyond the encounter of two persons in private and takes on the larger task of re-imagining the public world within which the patient lives (Ogilvy 1977). This notion of therapy attempts to realize the poetic basis of mind in actuality, as an imaginative, aesthetic response. When the environment is recognized as imagistic, then each person reacts to it in a more psychological manner, thereby extending both the notion of the 'psychological' to the aesthetic and the notion of therapy from occasional hours in the consulting room to a continual imaginative activity in the home, the street, while eating, or watching television.

Feeling

The liberation of therapy from the exclusivity of the consulting room first requires a re-evaluation of the identity psyche = feeling, that identification of the individual with emotion which has characterized all schools of psycho-therapy ever since Freud's work with conversion hysteria, emotional abreaction, and transference. In brief, therapy has

been concerned with personal feeling, and the patient's images have been reduced to his feelings. Hillman (1960,
1971), in two books devoted to emotion and to feeling, be-
gan a phenomenological and differentiated analysis of the
notions and theories of feeling and emotion as an avenue
toward releasing therapy, and psychology itself, from the
inevitable narrowing into personalism occasioned by the
identification of soul with feeling. The main argument
against the personal confessional mode of therapy (Hillman
1979c)—besides its perpetuating the Cartesian division of
ensouled subject/lifeless object—is that it fosters the delusion
of ownership of emotion, as belonging to the proprium
(Allport 1955). The intensified singleness that emotions
bring, their narrowing monocentristic effect upon consciousness,
gives support to the already monotheistic tendency of the
ego to appropriate and identify with its experiences. Emotions
reinforce ego psychology. Moreover, when emotion and feeling
are conceived as primary, images must play a secondary role.
They are considered to be derivative and descriptive of feelings.

Instead, archetypal psychology reverses the relation
of feeling and image: feelings are considered to be, as William
Blake said, "divine influxes," accompanying, qualifying, and
energizing images. They are not merely personal but belong to
imaginal reality, the reality of the image, and help make the
image felt as a specific value. Feelings elaborate its complexity, and feelings are as complex as the image that contains
them. Not images represent feelings, but feelings are inherent
to images. Berry (1974, 63) writes: "A dream image is or
has the quality of emotion . . . . They [emotions] adhere or
inhere to the image and may not be explicit at all . . . . We
cannot entertain any image in dreams, or poetry or painting,

without experiencing an emotional quality presented by the image itself." This further implies that any event experienced as an image is at once animated, emotionalized, and placed in the realm of value.

The task of therapy is to return personal feelings (anxiety, desire, confusion, boredom, misery) to the specific images which hold them. Therapy attempts to individualize the face of each emotion: the body of desire, the face of fear, the situation of despair. Feelings are imagined into their details. This move is similar to that of the imagist theory of poetry (Hulme 1924), where any emotion not differentiated by a specific image is inchoate, common, and dumb, remaining both sentimentally personal and yet collectively unindividualized.

13   Eros

Since its inception, depth psychology has consistently recognized the special role of eros in its work. In fact, psychoanalysis has been as much an eroto-analysis as an analysis of soul, since its basic perspective toward soul has been libidinal. The omnipresence of eros in therapy and in the theory of all depth psychologies receives this recognition under the technical term transference.

Archetypal psychology, analogously to Jung's alchemical psychology of transference, imagines transference against a mythical background—the Eros and Psyche mythologem from Apuleius's *Golden Ass* (Hillman 1972c, 63-125)— thereby de-historicizing and de-personalizing the phenomenology of love in therapy as well as in any human passion. "By recognizing the primacy of the image, archetypal thought frees both psyche and logos to an Eros that is imaginal" (Bedford 1981, 245). The imaginal, mythical transposition implies that all erotic phenomena whatsoever, including erotic symptoms, seek psychological consciousness and that all psychic phenomena whatsoever, including neurotic and psychotic symptoms, seek erotic embrace. Wherever psyche is the subject of endeavor or the perspective taken toward events, erotic entanglements will necessarily occur because the mythological tandem necessitates their appearance together. While Apuleius's myth details the obstacles in the relation between love and soul, Robert Stein (1974) has developed an archetypal approach to the incestuous family hindrances which prevent eros from becoming psychological and psyche from becoming erotic.

The idea of a mythic tandem as basis of transference was first suggested by Freud's Oedipal theory and elaborated by Jung in his anima/animus theory (*CW* 16). Archetypal psychology has gone on to describe a variety of tandems: Senex and Puer (Hillman 1967b); Venus and Vulcan (Murray Stein 1973); Pan and the Nymphs (Hillman 1972a); Apollo and Daphne; Apollo and Dionysus; Hermes and Apollo (Lopez–Pedraza 1977); Zeus and Hera (M. Stein 1977); Artemis and Puer (Moore 1979a); Echo and Narcissus (Berry 1979b); Demeter and Persephone (Berry 1975); Mother and Son (Hillman 1973b). Guggenbühl–Craig has discussed the archetypal fantasies operating in the patient–helper relationship (1971) and in the dyad of marriage (1977). These tandems provide occasion for the examination of diverse forms of erotic relationships, their rhetorics and expectations, the particular styles of suffering, and the interlocking mutualities that each tandem imposes. These tandems are imagined also as going on intra-psychically, as patterns of relations between complexes within an individual.

Since love of soul is also love of image, archetypal psychology considers transference, including its strongest sexualized demonstrations, to be a phenomenon of imagination. Nowhere does the impersonality of myth strike a human life more personally. Thus transference is the paradigm for working through the relations of personal and literal with the impersonal and imaginal. Transference is thus nothing less than the eros required by the awakening of psychic reality; and this awakening imposes archetypal roles upon patient and therapist, not the least of which is that of "psychological patient" which means one who suffers or is impassioned by psyche. For this erotic—not medical—reason, archetypal psychology retains the term "patient" instead of client, analysand, trainee, etc. The erotic struggles in any relationship are also psychological struggles with images, and as this *psychomachia* proceeds in an archetypal therapy, there is a transformation of love from a repression and/or obsession with images to a slow love of them, to a recognition that love is itself rooted in images, their continuous creative appearance and their love for that particular human soul in which they manifest.

14   *Personality Theory: Personifying*

Archetypal psychology's personality theory differs fundamentally from the main views of personality in Western psychology. If pathologizing belongs to the soul and is not to be combated by a strong ego, and if therapy (q.v.) consists in giving support to the counter-ego forces, the personified figures who are ego-alien, then both the theory of psychopathology and that of therapy assume a personality theory that is not ego-centered.

The first axiom of this theory is based on the late development of Jung's complex theory (1946) which holds that every personality is essentially multiple (*CW* 8, §388ff.). Multiple personality is humanity in its natural condition. In other cultures these multiple personalities have names, locations, energies, functions, voices, angel and animal forms, and even theoretical formulations as different kinds of soul. In our culture the multiplicity of personality is regarded either as a psychiatric aberration or, at best, as unintegrated introjections or partial personalities. The psychiatric fear of multiple personality indicates the identification of personality with a partial capacity, the "ego," which is in turn the psychological enactment of a two-thousand-year monotheistic tradition that has elevated unity over multiplicity.

Archetypal psychology extends Jung's personified naming of the components of personality—shadow, anima, animus, trickster, old wise man, great mother, etc. "Personifying or imagining things" (Hillman 1975a, 1-51) becomes crucial for moving from an abstract, objectified psychology to one that encourages animistic engagement with the world. Personifying further allows the multiplicity of psychic phenomena to be experienced as voices, faces, and names.

Psychic phenomena can then be perceived with precision and particularity, rather than generalized in the manner of faculty psychology as feelings, ideas, sensations, and the like.

For archetypal psychology, consciousness is given with the various "partial" personalities. Rather than being imagined as split-off fragments of the "I," they are better reverted to the differentiated models of earlier psychologies where the complexes would have been called souls, daimones, genii, and other mythical–imaginal figures. The consciousness that is postulated *a priori* with these figures or personifications is demonstrated by their interventions in ego control, i.e., the psychopathology of everyday life (Freud), disturbances of attention in the association experiments dung), the willfulness and aims of figures in dreams, the obsessive moods and compulsive thoughts that may intrude during any *abaissment du niveau mental* (Janet). Whereas most psychologies attempt to ban these personalities as disintegrative, archetypal psychology favors bringing non-ego figures to further awareness and considers this tension with the non-ego which relativizes the ego's surety and single perspective to be a chief occupation of soul–making (q.v.).

Thus, personality is conceived less in terms of stages in life and development, of typologies of character and functioning, of psycho-energetics toward goals (social, individual, etc.) or of faculties (will, affect, reason) and their balance. Rather, personality is imaginatively conceived as a living and peopled drama in which the subject "I" takes part but is neither the sole author, nor director, nor always the main character. Sometimes he or she is not even on the stage. At other times, the other theories of personality just reviewed may play their parts as necessary fictions for the drama.

The healthy or mature or ideal personality will thus show cognizance of its dramatically masked and ambiguous situation. Irony, humor, and compassion will be its hallmarks, since these traits bespeak an awareness of the multiplicity of meanings and fates and the multiplicity of intentions embodied by any subject at any moment. The "healthy personality" is imagined less upon a model of natural, primitive, or ancient man with its nostalgia, or upon social–political man with its mission, or bourgeois rational man with its moralism, but instead against the background of artistic man for whom imagining is a style of living and whose reactions are reflexive, animal, immediate. This model is, of course, not meant literally or singly. It serves to stress certain values of personality to which archetypal psychology gives importance: sophistication, complexity, and impersonal profundity; an animal flow with life disregarding concepts of will, choice, and decision; morality as dedication to crafting the soul (soul–making, q.v.); sensitivity to traditional continuities; the significance of pathologizing and living at the "borders;" aesthetic responsiveness.

15 *Biographical*

As shown above, archetypal psychology is not a theoretical system emanating from the thought of one person for whom it is named, then identifying with a small group, becoming a school, and moving into the world in the manner of Freudian or Jungian psychologies; nor does it emerge from a particular clinic, laboratory, or city giving it its name. Rather, archetypal psychology presents the polytheistic structure of a post-modern consciousness. It is a style of thinking, a fashion of mind, a revisionist engagement on many fronts: therapy, education, literary criticism, medicine, philosophy, and the material world. It assembles and lends its terms and viewpoints to a variety of intellectual concerns in contemporary thought. Eros (q.v.) and a common concern for soul, image, and pathology draw individuals from diverse geographical and intellectual areas into rapport with each other for the revisioning of their ideas and their worlds.

Inasmuch as the sources (q.v.) are in Jung and Corbin, the biographical origins can be traced to the Eranos Conferences at Ascona, Switzerland (Rudolf Ritsema), where Jung and Corbin were perennially major speakers; Durand and Hillman entered that circle in the 1960s, Miller in the 1970s, and Giegerich in 1982. The Platonist inspiration at Eranos, its concern for spirit in a time of crisis and decay, the mutuality of engagement that transcends academic specialization, and the educative effect of eros on soul were together formative in the directions that archetypal psychology was subsequently to take.

A second biographical strand can be discerned in a period (April 1969) at the Warburg Institute in London and the confrontation by Raphael Lopez–Pedraza, James Hillman, and Patricia Berry with the tradition of classical (pagan, polytheistic) images in the Western psyche. Here they found witness to a ground for psychology in the cultural imagination, especially of the Mediterranean, which would allow psychology to return from its distractions by natural science and Eastern spirituality. Third was the re-founding

(1970) in Zürich of the formerly Jungian journal *Spring* as an organ of archetypal thought and the launching of other publications, as well as seminars on psychological readings of Renaissance images.

Fourth, subsequent developments took place in the Western Hemisphere. In February 1972 the invitation to give the distinguished Dwight Harrington Terry Lectures at Yale University enabled Hillman (1975a) to present the first comprehensive formulation of archetypal psychology. This was followed by the appointment of Hillman and Berry as visiting lecturers in the Yale psychology faculty, where their association with the Yale philosopher Edward Casey turned their work toward mutual explorations of the philosophy of imagination and phenomenology. During the mid-seventies, graduate degree programs were being established at Sonoma State, California (Gordon Tappan), and the University of Dallas (Robert Sardello). In 1976 Hillman and Berry joined the faculty of the Department of Religions at Syracuse University, New York, and in collaboration with David Miller worked further into the problems of monotheistic and polytheistic thinking. In January 1977, partly sponsored by a grant from the Rockefeller Brothers Foundation, archetypal psychology held its first International Seminar at the University of Dallas, gathering together some twenty of the individuals mentioned in this article. Other conferences and seminars were held at the University of Notre Dame, Indiana (Thomas Kapacinskas), Duquesne University, Pennsylvania, and the University of New Mexico (Howard McConeghey). In January 1978, the University of Dallas appointed Hillman Professor of Psychology and Senior Fellow in the Institute of Philosophic Studies (Robert Sardello) and Berry as Visiting Professor.

Meanwhile, Lopez–Pedraza had been appointed Lecturer in mythology and psychology in the Faculty of Letters at the University of Caracas. With the opening (1981) of the Dallas Institute of Humanities and Culture (whose Fellows include Sardello, Thomas, Moore, Stroud, Berry, Hillman, and Guggenbühl–Craig), archetypal psychology turned toward the "soul in the world" (*anima mundi*) of the city. "City" becomes the patient, the place of pathologizing, and the locus where the soul's imagination is actualized on earth, requiring an archetypally psychological perspective for examining its ills.

No nation in Europe has responded more attentively to this re-visionist thought than Italy. A number of engaged intellectuals and therapists in Rome, Florence, Pisa, and Milan have succeeded in translating (Aldo Giuliani) works of archetypal psychology in the *Rivista di psicologia analitica*, in books (Adelphi, Communitá), and in publications of the Enciclopedia Italiana and have presented its thought in teaching, editing, and translating (Francesco Donfrancesco, Bianca Garufi). In France, a similar initiative, joining with the groups affiliated with Henry Corbin and Gilbert Durand, was pioneered by Editions Imago, by Michel Cazenave and by Monique Salzmann.

Two recent European events—a world conference in Cordoba on "Science and Consciousness" (Cazenave 1980), reflecting the thought of Jung and Corbin and the Eranos circle (Miller, Izutsu, Durand, Raine, Hillman) in relation with contemporary physical sciences, and an address by Hillman (1982) on archetypal psychology as a Renaissance psychology in Florence (Donfrancesco)—have presented what is reviewed in this essay in the wide current of contemporary Western ideas.

Part Two

References

Nota bene: All references to *Spring: A Journal of Archetype and Culture* (formerly subtitled *An Annual of Archetypal Psychology and Jungian Thought*) have been given by year and pages; the publisher is Spring Publications, at times located in New York, Zürich, Irving and Dallas, Texas, and Putnam and Woodstock, Connecticut. Within the text all references to C. G. Jung follow the the standard abbreviation of his *Collected Works* (*CW*, volume number, paragraph number), published by Princeton University Press and by Routledge and Kegan Paul, London. Each bibliography entry includes after the author's name the date that appears in the text when that source is cited.

Allport, Gordon (1955). *Becoming* (The Terry Lectures). New Haven: Yale University Press, 1955.

Armstrong, A. H. (1981). "Some Advantages of Polytheism." *Dionysius 5* (1981): 181-88.

Armstrong, Robert P. (1971). *The Affecting Presence*. Urbana: University of Illinois Press, 1971.

Avens, Roberts (1980). *Imagination Is Reality: Western Nirvana in Jung, Hillman, Barfield and Cassirer*. Dallas: Spring Publications, 1980.

_____ (1982a). "Heidegger and Archetypal Psychology." *International Philosophical Quarterly* 22 (1982): 183-202.

_____ (1982b). *Imaginal Body: Para-Jungian Reflections on Soul, Imagination and Death.* Washington, D. C.: University Press of America, 1982.

Bachelard, Gaston (1943). *L'Air et les songes.* Paris: Corti, 1943.

Bedford, Gary S. (1981). "Notes on Mythological Psychology." *Journal of the American Academy of Religion* 49 (1981): 231-47.

*Berry, Patricia (1973). "On Reduction." *Spring 1973*: 67-84.

_____ (1974). "An Approach to the Dream." *Spring 1974*: 58-79.

_____ (1975). "The Rape of Demeter/Persephone and Neurosis." *Spring 1975*: 186-98.

_____ (1978a). "Defense and Telos in Dreams." *Spring 1978*: 115-27.

_____ (1978b). *What's the Matter with Mother?* Pamphlet, London: Guild of Pastoral Psychology, 1978.

_____ (1979a). "Virginities of Image." Paper: *Dragonflies* Conference on Virginity in Psyche, Myth, and Community, University of Dallas, 1979.

_____ (1979b). "Echo's Passion." Paper: *Dragonflies* Conference on Beauty in Psyche, Myth, and Community, University of Dallas, 1979.

_____ (1981). "The training of shadow and the shadow of training." *Journal of Analytical Psychology* 26 (1981): 221-28.

_____ (1982). "Hamlet's Poisoned Ear." *Spring 1982*: 195-210.

Boer, Charles, trans. (1980). *Marsilio Ficino: The Book of Life.* Spring Publications, 1980.

_____ and Kugler, Peter (1977). "Archetypal Psychology Is Mythical Realism." *Spring 1977*: 131-52.

---

*The papers of Patricia Berry subsequently have been collected in one volume, *Echo's Subtle Body*, Dallas: Spring Publications, 1982.

Bregman, Lucy (1980). "Religious Imagination: Polytheistic Psychology Confronts Calvin." *Soundings* 63 (1980): 36-60.

Casey, Edward S. (1974). "Toward an Archetypal Imagination." *Spring 1974*: 1-32.

_____ (1976). *Imagining: A Phenomenological Study.* Bloomington: University of Indiana Press, 1976.

_____ (1979). "Time in the Soul." *Spring 1979*: 144-64.

_____ (1982). "Getting Placed: Soul in Space." *Spring 1982*:1-25.

Cazenave, Michel (1980). *Science et Conscience.* Paris: Stock, 1980.

Christou, Evangelos (1963). *The Logos of the Soul.* Zürich: Spring Publications, 1963.

Cook, Daniel J. (1973). *Language in the Philosophy of Hegel*, 62. The Hague: Mouton, 1973.

Corbin, Henry (1958). *L'Imagination créatrice dans le Soufisme d'Ibn'Arab*i. Paris: Flammarion, 1958 [in translation: *Creative Imagination in the Sufism of Ibn 'Arabi.* Bollingen Series, vol. 91. Princeton: Princeton University Press, 1969].

_____ (1971-73). *En Islam iranien.* 4 vols. Paris: Gallimard, 1971-73.

_____ (1977). *Spiritual Body and Celestial Earth.* Bollingen Series. Princeton: Princeton University Press, 1977.

_____ (1979). *Avicenne et le récit visionnaire.* Paris: Berg International, 2d ed., 1979 [in translation: *Avicenna and the Visionary Recital.* Dallas: Spring Publications, 1980].

Cowan, Lyn (1979). "On Masochism." *Spring 1979*: 42-54.

Durand, Gilbert (1960). *Les Structures anthropologiques de l'imaginaire: introduction a l'archetypologie generale.* Paris: Bordas, 6th ed., 1979.

_____ (1975). *Science de l'homme et tradition*. Paris: Berg International, 1975.

_____ (1979). *Figures mythiques et visages de l'oeuvre*. Paris: Berg International, 1979.

Frey-Wehrlin, C. T., Bosnak, R. et al. (1978). "The Treatment of Chronic Psychosis." *Journal of Analytical Psychology* 23 (1978): 253-57.

Garufi, Bianca (1977). "Reflections on the 'rêve éveillé dirigé' method." *Journal of Analytical Psychology* 22 (1977): 207-29.

Giegerich, Wolfgang (1977). "On the Neurosis of Psychology." *Spring 1977*: 153-74.

_____ (1982). "Busse für Philemon: Vertiefung in das verdorbene Gast-Spiel der Götter." In *Eranos Jahrbuch 51-1982*.

Goldenberg, Naomi (1975). "Archetypal Theory after Jung." *Spring 1975*: 199-220.

_____ (1979). *Changing of the Gods: Feminism and the End of Traditional Religion*. Boston: Beacon, 1979.

Grinnell, Robert (1973). *Alchemy in a Modern Woman*. Zürich: Spring Publications, 1973.

Guggenbühl-Craig, Adolf (1970). "Must Analysis Fail through Its Destructive Aspect?" *Spring 1970*: 133-45.

(1971). *Macht als Gefahr beim Helfer*. Basel: Karger, 1971 [in translation: *Power in the Helping Professions*. Zürich: Spring Publications, 1971].

_____ (1972). "Analytical Rigidity and Ritual." *Spring 1972*: 34-42.

_____ (1977). *Marriage-Dead or Alive*. Zürich: Spring Publications, 1977.

_____ (1979). "The Archetype of the Invalid and the Limits of Healing." *Spring 1979*: 29-41.

Hartman, Gary V. (1980). "Psychotherapy: An Attempt at Definition." *Spring 1980*: 90-100.

Hawkins, Ernest (1979). "On Migraine-From Dionysos to Freud." *Dragonflies: Studies in Imaginal Psychology* 1 (1979): 46-69.

Hillman, James (1960). *Emotion: A comprehensive phenomenology of theories and their meanings for therapy.* London: Routledge & Kegan Paul, 1960.

_____ (1964). *Suicide and the Soul.* New York: Harper, 1964 [reprinted; Zürich/Woodstock: Spring Publications, 1976, 1997].

_____ (1967a). *Insearch: Psychology and Religion.* London: Hodder and Stoughton, 1967 [reprinted; Dallas/Woodstock: Spring Publications, 1979, 1994].

_____ (1967b). "Senex and Puer." In *Puer Papers*, 3-53. Spring Publications, 1979.

_____ (1970a). "On Senex Consciousness." *Spring 1970*: 146-65.

_____ (1970b). "Why 'Archetypal' Psychology?" *Spring 1970*: 212-19.

_____ (1971). "The Feeling Function." In *Lectures on Jung's Typology* (with M.-L. von Franz), 74-150. Zürich: Spring Publications, 1971.

_____ (1972a). "An Essay on Pan." In *Pan and the Nightmare* (with W. H. Roscher), i-lxiii. Zürich: Spring Publications, 1972.

_____ (1972b). "Failure and Analysis." *Journal of Analytical Psychology* 17 (1972): 1-6.

_____ (1972c). *The Myth of Analysis.* Evanston, Ill.: Northwestern University Press, 1972.

_____ (1973a). "Plotino, Ficino e Vico precursori della psicologia degli archetipi." *Rivista di psicologia analitica* 4 (1973): 322-40.

_____ (1973b). "The Great Mother, Her Son, Her Hero, and the Puer." In *Fathers and Mothers: Five Papers on the Archetypal Background of Family Psychology*, edited by Patricia Berry, 75-127. Zürich: Spring Publications, 1973 [reprinted and revised; Dallas, 1991].

_____ (1973c). "Anima." *Spring 1973*: 97-132.

_____ (1974a). "On the Necessity of Abnormal Psychology." In *Eranos Jahrbuch 43-1974*, 91-135. Leiden: E. J. Brill, 1977.

_____ (1974b). "'Anima' (II)." *Spring 1974*: 113-46.

_____ (1975a). *Re-Visioning Psychology.* New York: Harper, 1975.

_____ (1975b). *Loose Ends: Primary Papers in Archetypal Psychology.* Zürich: Spring Publications, 1975.

_____ (1975c). "The Fiction of Case History." In *Religion as Story*, edited by J. B. Wiggins, 123-73. New York: Harper, 1975.

_____ (1975d). "The 'Negative' Senex and a Renaissance Solution." *Spring 1975*: 7-109.

_____ (1976). "Peaks and Vales: The Soul/Spirit Distinction as Basis for the Differences between Psychotherapy and Spiritual Discipline." In *On the Way to Self-Knowledge*, edited by J. Needleman and D. Lewis, 114-47. New York: Knopf, 1976 [reprinted: in *Puer Papers*, 54-74. Dallas: Spring Publications, 1979].

_____ (1977a). "The Pandaemonium of Images: C. G. Jung's Contribution to *Know Thyself*." *New Lugano Review* 3 (1977): 35-45.

_____ (1977b). "An Inquiry into Image." *Spring 1977*: 62-88.

_____ (1977c). "Psychotherapy's Inferiority Complex." In *Eranos Jahrbuch 46-1977*, 121-74. Frankfurt a/M: Insel Verlag, 1981.

_____ (1978). "Further Notes on Images." *Spring 1978*: 152-82.

_____ (1979a). *The Dream and the Underworld.* New York: Harper, 1979.

_____ (1979b). "Image-Sense." *Spring 1979*: 130-43.

_____ (1979c). "The Thought of the Heart." In *Eranos Jahrbuch 48-1979*, 133-82. Frankfurt a/M: Insel Verlag, 1981.

_____ (1981a). "Silver and the White Earth (Part Two)." *Spring 1981*: 21-66.

_____ (1981b). "Alchemical Blue and the Unio Mentalis." *Sulfur* 1 (1981): 33-50.

_____ (1982). *"Anima mundi*: The Return of the Soul to the World." *Spring 1982:* 71-93.

_____ and Berry, Patricia (1977). "Archetypal Therapy." Paper: First International Seminar of Archetypal Psychology, University of Dallas, Irving, Texas, 1977.

Hough, Graham (1973). "Poetry and the Anima." *Spring 1973*: 85-96.

Hull, R. F. C. (1971). "Bibliographical Notes on Active Imagination in the Works of C. G. Jung." *Spring 1971*: 115-20.

Hulme, T. E. (1924). *Speculations*. London: Routledge, 1924.

Humbert, Elie (1971). "Active Imagination: Theory and Practice." *Spring 1971*: 101-14.

James, William (1909). *A Pluralistic Universe*. London, 1909.

Jung, C. G. *The Collected Works (CW)*. Translated by R. F. C. Hull. Bollingen Series XX, vols. 1-20, paragraph nos. Princeton: Princeton University Press, 1953 ff.

Jung, Emma (1957). *Animus and Anima*. Zürich: Spring Publications, 1957 [reprinted; Woodstock, 1997].

Kelly, George (1955). *The Psychology of Personal Constructs*. 2 vols. New York: Norton, 1955.

Kugelmann, Robert. *The Windows of Soul: Psychological Physiology of the Human Eye and Primary Glaucoma*. Lewisburg, Pennsylvania: Bucknell University Press, forthcoming.

Kugler, Paul K. (1978). "Image and Sound." *Spring 1978*: 136-51.

_____ (1979a). "The Phonetic Imagination." *Spring 1979*: 118-29.

_____ (1979b). *The Alchemy of Discourse: An Archetypal Approach to Language*. Dissertation, C. G. Jung Institute, Zürich, 1979 [Lewisburg, Pennsylvania: Bucknell University Press, 1982].

Leveranz, John (1979). "The Sacred Disease." *Dragonflies: Studies in Imaginal Psychology* 1 (1979): 18-38.

Lockhart, Russell A. (1977). "Cancer in Myth and Disease." *Spring 1977*: 1-26.

_____ (1978). "Words as Eggs." *Dragonflies: Studies in Imaginal Psychology* 1 (1978): 3-32.

_____ (1980). "Psyche in Hiding." *Quadrant* 13 (1980): 76-105.

Lopez-Pedraza, Rafael (1977). *Hermes and His Children*. Zürich: Spring Publications, 1977.

_____ (1982). "Moon Madness-Titanic Love: A Meeting of Pathology and Poetry." In *Images of the Untouched*, edited by Joanne Stroud and Gail Thomas, 11-26. Dallas: Spring Publications, 1982.

McConeghey, Howard (1981). "Art Education and Archetypal Psychology." *Spring 1981*: 127-35.

Micklem, Niel (1979). "The Intolerable Image: The Mythic Background of Psychosis." *Spring 1979*: 1-18.

Miller, David L. (1972). "Polytheism and Archetypal Theology." *Journal of the American Academy of Religion* 40 (1972): 513-27.

_____ (1974). *The New Polytheism*. New York: Harper, 1974 [reissued: with appendix "Psychology: Monotheistic or Polytheistic" (James Hillman). Dallas: Spring Publications, 1981].

_____ (1976a). "Fairy Tale or Myth." *Spring 1976*: 157-64.

_____ (1976b). "Mythopoesis, Psychopoesis, Theopoesis: The Poetries of Meaning." Panarion Conference tape, 1976.

_____ (1977). "Imaginings No End." In *Eranos Jahrbuch 46-1977*, 451-500. Leiden: E. J. Brill, 1981.

_____ (1981a). *Christs: Meditations on Archetypal Images in Christian Theology*. New York: The Seabury Press, 1981.

_____ (1981b). "The Two Sandals of Christ: Descent into History and into Hell." In *Eranos Jahrbuch 50-1981*, 147-221. Frankfurt a/M: Insel Verlag, 1982.

Moore, Tom (1978). "Musical Therapy." *Spring 1978*: 128-35.

_____ (1979a). "Artemis and the Puer." In *Puer Papers*, 169-204. Dallas: Spring Publications, 1979.

_____ (1979b). "Images in Asthma: Notes for a Study of Disease." *Dragonflies: Studies in Imaginal Psychology* 1 (1979): 3-14.

_____ (1980). "James Hillman: Psychology with Soul." *Religious Studies Review* 6 (1980): 278-84.

_____ (1982). *The Planets Within*. Lewisburg, Pennsylvania: Bucknell University Press, 1982.

Newman, K. D. (1980). "Counter-Transference and Consciousness." *Spring 1980*: 117-27.

Ogilvy, James (1977). *Many-Dimensional Man: Decentralizing Self, Society and the Sacred*. New York: Oxford University Press, 1977.

Ritsema, Rudolf (1976). "On the Syntax of the Imaginal." *Spring 1976*: 191-94.

Romanyshyn, Robert (1977). "Remarks on the Metaphorical Basis of Psychological Life." Paper: First International Seminar on Archetypal Psychology, University of Dallas, 1977.

_____ (1978-79). "Psychological Language and the Voice of Things" (I and II). *Dragonflies: Studies in Imaginal Psychology* 1 (1978, 1979): 74-90, 73-79.

Sardello, Robert J. (1978a). "Ensouling Language." *Dragonflies: Studies in Imaginal Psychology* 1 (1978): 1-2.

_____ (1978b). "An Empirical-Phenomenological Study of Fantasy." *Psychocultural Review* 2 (1978).

_____ (1979a). "Imagination and the Transformation of the Perceptual World." Paper: Third American Conference on Fantasy and the Imaging Process, New York, 1979.

_____ (1979b). *Educating with Soul.* Pamphlet, Center for Civic Leadership, University of Dallas, 1979.

_____ (1980a). "The Mythos of Medicine." In *Medicine and Literature*, edited by K. Rabuzzi. Austin: University of Texas Press, forthcoming.

_____ (1980b). "Beauty and Violence: The Play of Imagination in the World." *Dragonflies: Studies in Imaginal Psychology* 2 (1980): 91-104.

_____ et al. (1978). *Dragonflies: Studies in Imaginal Psychology* 1 (1978).

Scott, Charles E. (1980). "On Hillman and Calvin." *Soundings* 63 (1980): 61-73.

Severson, Randolph (1978). "Titans Under Glass: A Recipe for the Recovery of Psychological Jargon." *Dragonflies: Studies in Imaginal Psychology* 1 (1978): 64-73.

_____ (1979). "Puer's Wounded Wing: Reflections on the Psychology of Skin Disease." In *Puer Papers*, 129-51. Dallas: Spring Publications, 1979.

Simmer, Stephen (1981). "The Academy of the Dead: On Boredom, Writer's Block, Footnotes and Deadlines." *Spring 1981*: 89-106.

Sipiora, Michael P. (1981). "A Soul's Journey: Camus, Tuberculosis, and Aphrodite." *Spring 1981*: 163-76.

Stein, Murray (1973). "Hephaistos: A Pattern of Introversion." *Spring 1973*: 35-51.

_____ (1977). "Hera: Bound and Unbound." *Spring 1977*: 105-19.

Stein, Robert (1974). *Incest and Human Love.* Baltimore:

Penguin, 1974 [reprinted; Dallas: Spring Publications, 1984].

Vico, Giambattista. *Scienza Nuova*. Napoli, 1744 [in translation: *The New Science*. Ithaca: Cornell University Press, 1968].

Vitale, Augusto (1973). "Saturn: The Transformation of the Father." In *Fathers and Mothers: Five Papers on the Archetypal Background of Family Psychology*, edited by Patricia Berry, 5-39. Zürich: Spring Publications, 1973[reprinted and revised; Dallas, 1991].

de Voogd, Stephanie (1977). "C. G. Jung: Psychologist of the Future, 'Philosopher' of the Past." *Spring 1977*: 175-82.

Watkins, Mary M. (1976). *Waking Dreams*. New York: Gordon & Breach, 1976 [reprinted; Dallas: Spring Publications: 1984].

_____ (1981). "Six Approaches to the Image in Art Therapy." *Spring 1981*: 107-25.

Wind, Edgar (1967). *Pagan Mysteries in the Renaissance*. Harmondsworth, England: Peregrine, 1967.

Winquist, Charles (1981). "The Epistemology of Darkness." *Journal of the American Academy of Religion* 49 (1981): 23-34.

Yates, Frances (1966). *The Art of Memory*. London: Routledge, 1966.

Ziegler, A. J. (1980). *Morbismus: Archetypisches Medizin*. Zürich: Raben Reihe, Schweizer Spiegel Verlag, 1980 [in translation: *Archetypal Medicine*. Dallas, Texas: Spring Publications, 1983].

Part Three

Complete Checklist of Works by James Hillman
(through January 1997)

A. Books and Monographs
B. Collaborative Volumes
C. Edited Volumes
D. Published Essays and Lectures
E. Contributions to the Eranos Jahrbuch
F. Prefaces and Occasional Writings
G. Unpublished Writings
H. Interviews

Translations of A-H
Czech
Danish
Dutch
French
German
Hungarian
Italian
Japanese
Polish
Portuguese
Russian
Spanish
Swedish

A. Books and Monographs

A60   *Emotion: A Comprehensive Phenomenology of Theories and Their Meanings for Therapy.* London:
Routledge & Kegan Paul, 1960, and Evanston, Ill.:
Northwestern University Press, 1961, [revised 1964;
with new a preface 1992].

A64   *Suicide and the Soul.* London: Hodder and Stoughton,
and New York: Harper, 1964; Harper Colophon edition, 1973, [reprinted; Dallas: Spring Publications,
1976, Woodstock, Conn., 1997].

A67   *Insearch: Psychology and Religion.* London: Hodder
and Stoughton, and New York: Charles Scribner's
Sons, 1967 [reprinted; Dallas: Spring Publications,
1979, Woodstock, Conn., 1996].

A72   *The Myth of Analysis: Three Essays in Archetypal Psychology.* Evanston: Northwestern University Press,
1972. [reprinted; Harper Colophon edition, New
York: Harper, 1978; Harper Perennial, 1992].

A75a *Loose Ends: Primary Papers in Archetypal Psychology.*
New York / Zürich: Spring Publications, 1975 [re-
printed; Dallas, 1981].

A75b *Re-Visioning Psychology.* New York: Harper, 1975;
Harper Colophon edition, 1977; [reprinted; Harper
Perennial, 1992, with new preface (F92b)]. Excerpts
as "Soul and Spirit" appeared in *Common Boundary* (November-December 1992): 32-33.

A79   *The Dream and the Underworld.* New York: Harper, 1979.

A83a *Healing Fiction.* Barrytown, New York: Station Hill
Press, 1983 [reprinted; Woodstock, Conn.: Spring
Publications, 1996].

A83b *Archetypal Psychology: A Brief Account.* Dallas: Spring
      Publications, 1983 [reprinted with an addendum to
      the Checklist 1985; revised Checklist 1988, 1993,
      and Woodstock, Conn., 1997].
A84   *The Thought of the Heart.* Eranos Lectures Series 2.
      Dallas: Spring Publications, 1984.
A85   *Anima: An Anatomy of a Personified Notion* (with excerpts
      from the writings of C. G. Jung and original drawings
      by Mary Vernon). Dallas: Spring Publications, 1985
      [reprinted; Woodstock, Conn., 1996].
A86   *Egalitarian Typologies versus the Perception of the
      Unique.* Eranos Lectures Series 4. Dallas: Spring
      Publications, 1986.
A88   *On Paranoia.* Eranos Lectures Series 8. Dallas:
      Spring Publications, 1988.
A92   *The Thought of the Heart and the Soul of the World.*
      Dallas: Spring Publications, 1992 [reprinted;
      Woostock, Conn., 1996].
A95   *Kinds of Power: A Guide to its Intelligent Uses.* New
      York: Doubleday/Currency, 1995.
A96   *The Soul's Code: In Search of Character and Calling.*
      New York: Random House, 1996.

B. Collaborative Volumes

B67   "A Psychological Commentary" to *Kundalini: The Evolu-
      tionary Energy in Man,* by Gopi Krishna. New Delhi /
      Zürich: Ramadhar and Hopman, 1967. London: Stuart
      and Watkins, and Berkeley: Shambhala, 1970.
B71   "The Feeling Function." In *Lectures on Jung's Typology*

(with "The Inferior Function," by Marie-Louise von Franz), 89-182. New York / Zürich: Spring Publications, 1971 [reprinted; Dallas, 1986, Woodstock, Conn., 1996].

B72   "An Essay on Pan." In *Pan and the Nightmare* (with "Ephialtes: A Pathological-Mythological Treatise on the Nightmare in Classical Antiquity," by W. H. Roscher), 3-65, 156. New York / Zürich: Spring Publications, 1972 [reprinted; Dallas, 1988, revised edition; Woodstock, Conn., 1997].

B83   *Inter Views: Conversations between James Hillman and Laura Pozzo on Therapy, Biography, Love, Soul, Dreams, Work, Imagination and the State of the Culture.* New York: Harper, 1983 [reprinted; Dallas: Spring Publications, 1991, Woodstock, Conn., 1996].

B85   *Freud's Own Cookbook* (with Charles Boer). New York: Harper, 1985.

B89   *A Blue Fire: Selected Writings by James Hillman.* Intro duced and edited by Thomas Moore in collaboration with the author. New York: Harper, 1989; Harper Perennial, 1991; London: Routledge, 1990, as *The Essential James Hillman.*

B91   "Oedipus Revisited." In *Oedipus Variations: Studies in Literature and Psychoanalysis* (with "Oedipus: Two Essays," by Karl Kerényi), 87-169. Dallas: Spring Publications, 1991 [reprinted; Woodstock, Conn., 1995].

B92   *We've Had a Hundred Years of Psychotherapy and the World's Getting Worse* (with Michael Ventura). HarperSanFrancisco, 1992. Excerpts appeared in *New Age Journal* (May-June 1992): 60-65, 136-41; in *LA Weekly,* May 22-28, 1992, 18-28; in *The*

Phoenix 12/9 (1992): 2, 5, 13; in *The Family Therapy Networker* (Nov-Dec 1992): 38-43; and in *Resurgence* 155, Bideford, Devon, England (Nov.-Dec. 1992): 32-33.

C. Edited Volumes

C(1) (Associate Editor). *Envoy: An Irish Review of Literature and Art.* 16 issues. Dublin, 1949-51.

C(2) *Students' Association Publications of the C. G. Jung Institute.* 3 pamphlets. Zürich, 1957-58.

C(3) *Studies in Jungian Thought.* 11 vols. Evanston: Northwestern University Press, 1967-74; Lewisburg, Penn.: Bucknell University Press, 1979- .

C(4) *Spring: An Annual of Archetypal Psychology and Jungian Thought.* New York, Zürich, Irving, Texas, Dallas, 1970-87.

C(5) *Spring: A Journal of Archetype and Culture.* Dallas, Putnam, Conn., Woodstock, Conn., 1988- .

C63 *The Logos of the Soul,* by Evangelos Christou. Vienna / Zürich: Dunquin Press, 1963 [reprinted; Dallas: Spring Publications, 1987].

C79 *Puer Papers.* Dallas: Spring Publications, 1979.

C80 *Facing the Gods.* Dallas: Spring Publications, 1980 [reprinted; 1992].

C92 *The Rag and Bone Shop of the Heart: Poems for Men* (with Robert Bly and Michael Meade). New York: Harper, 1992.

D. Published Essays and Lectures

D62a "Friends and Enemies." *Harvest* 8 (1962): 1-22.

D62b "Training and the C. G. Jung Institute, Zürich," "A Note on Multiple Analysis and Emotional Climate in Training Institutes," and "Reply to Discussions" *Journal of Analytical Psychology* 7, London (1962): 3-22, 27-28.

 D63 "Methodologische Probleme in der Traumforschung." Translated by Hilde Binswanger. In *Traum und Symbol*, edited by C. A. Meier, 91-121 (Zürich: Rascher Verlag, 1963). Collected in English without bibliography in A75a.

D64 "Betrayal." Lecture 128, London: Guild of Pastoral Psychology, 1964. Reprinted in *Spring 1965*: 57-76 and in A75a.

D66 "Towards the Archetypal Model for the Masturbation Inhibition." *Journal of Analytical Psychology* 11/1, London (1966): 49-62. Reprinted in *The Reality of the Psyche*, edited by Joseph Wheelwright (New York: Putnam's, 1968), and in A75a.

D68 "C. G. Jung on Emotion." In *The Nature of Emotion*, edited by M. B. Arnold, 125-34 (Harmondsworth, England: Penguin Books, 1968).

D70a "C. G. Jung's Contribution to Feelings and Emotions: Synopsis and Implications." In *Feelings and Emotions*, edited by M. B. Arnold, 125-35 (New York: Academic Press, 1970).

D70b "An Imaginal Ego." In *Inscape* 2, 2-8 (London: British Association of Art Therapists, 1970).

D70c "On Senex Consciousness." *Spring 1970*: 146-65. Reprinted in *Fathers and Mothers*, 2nd edition, edited by Patricia Berry, 18-36 (Dallas: Spring Publications, 1990).

D70d "Why 'Archetypal' Psychology?" *Spring 1970*: 212-19. Reprinted with a postscript in A75a.

D71a "Psychology: Monotheistic or Polytheistic?" *Spring 1971*: 193-208, 230-32. Expanded in an Appendix to *The New Polytheism*, by David Miller, 109-42 (Dallas: Spring Publications, 1981).

D71b. "On the Psychology of Parapsychology." In *A Century of Psychical Research*, edited by A. Angoff and B. Shapin, 176-87 (New York: Parapsychology Foundation, 1971). Reprinted in A75a.

D72a "Dionysus in Jung's Writings." *Spring 1972*: 191-205. Reprinted in C80, 151-64.

D72b "Three Ways of Failure and Analysis." *Journal of Analytical Psychology*, 17/1, London (1972): 1-6. Reprinted in *Success and Failure in Analysis*, edited by G. Adler (New York: Putnam's, 1974), and in A75a.

D72c "Schism: As Differing Visions." Lecture 162. London: Guild of Pastoral Psychology, 1972. Reprinted in A75a.

D73a "Anima." *Spring 1973*: 97-132. Expanded in A85.

D73b "Pathologizing (or Falling Apart)." *Art International* 17/6, Lugano (1973). Revised in A75b.

D73c "The Great Mother, Her Son, Her Hero, and the Puer." In *Fathers and Mothers: Five Papers on the Archetypal Background of Family Psychology*, edited by P. Berry, 75-127 (New York / Zürich: Spring Publications, 1973). Second revised edition, 1990: 166-209.

D73d "Plotino, Ficino e Vico, precursori della psicologia degli archetipi." *Rivista di psicologia analitica* 4/2 (1973): 322-40. Reprinted in Italian and English in *Enciclopedia 1974* (Roma: Istituto della Enciclopedia Italiana, 1974), 67-80. Collected (in English) in A75a. Also in *L'anima del mondo e il pensiero del cuore* (Milano: Garzanti, 1993).

D74a "'Anima' (II)." *Spring 1974*: 113-46. Expanded in A85.

D74b "A Note on Story." *Children's Literature* 3 (1974): 9-11. Reprinted in *Parabola 4* (1979): 43-45. Collected in A75a. Also in *Reclaiming the Inner Child*, edited by J. Abrams, 277-79 (Los Angeles: Tarcher, 1990).

D74c "Archetypal Theory: C. G. Jung." In *Operational Theories of Personality*, edited by A. Burton, 65-98 (New York: Brunner/Mazel, 1974). Abridged in A75a.

D74d "Pothos: The Nostalgia of the Puer Eternus." Lecture first delivered in French, May 1974, in Chambéry. Collected (in English) in A75a.

D75a "The Fiction of Case History: A Round." In *Religion as Story*, edited by J. B. Wiggins, 123-73 (New York: Harper, 1975). Revised in A83a.

D75b "The 'Negative' Senex and a Renaissance Solution." *Spring 1975*: 77-109.

D76a "Peaks and Vales: The Soul/Spirit Distinction as Basis for the Differences between Psychotherapy and Spiritual Discipline." In *On the Way to Self-Knowledge*, edited by J. Needleman and D. Lewis, 114-47 (New York: Knopf, 1976). Collected in C79, 54-74.

D76b "Some Early Background to Jung's Ideas: Notes on *C. G. Jung's Medium* by Stefanie Zumstein-Preiswerk." *Spring 1976*: 123-36.

D77a "An Inquiry into Image." *Spring 1977*: 62-88.

D77b "The Pandaemonium of Images: C. G. Jung's Contribution to Know Thyself." *Art International* 3, Lugano (1977): 35-45. Revised in A83a. First published in German, E75.

D78a *City and Soul.* Irving, Texas: Center for Civic Leadership, University of Dallas, 1978. Reprinted in *Vision Magazine* (October 1978): 27-29. Reprinted in *Dromenon* 4 (1982): 57-59, in *Tarrytown Letter* 25 (The Tarrytown Group) (1983), and in *Urban Resources* 1/4 (1984): 36 and 42.

D78b "Further Notes on Images." *Spring 1978*: 152-82.

D78c "Therapeutic Value of Alchemical Language" *Dragonflies: Studies in Imaginal Psychology* 1/1 (1978): 33-42. Reprinted in *Methods of Treatment in Analytical Psychology*, edited by I. F. Baker, 118-26 (Fellbach: Verlag Adolf Bonz, 1980).

D79a "Image-Sense." *Spring 1979*: 130-43.

D79b "Notes on Opportunism." In C79, 152-65.

D79c "Puer's Wound and Ulysses' Scar." In C79, 100-28. Reprinted in *Dromenon* 3 (1981): 12-27.

D79d *Psychological Fantasies in Transportation Problems.* Irving, Texas: Center for Civic Leadership, University of Dallas, 1979.

D80a "La mesure des évènements: la proposition 117 de Proclus dans la perspective d'une psychologie archétypique." In *Science et Conscience*, edited by M. Cazenave, 238-99 (Paris: Stock, 1980).

D80b "Take a Walk." _D Magazine_ (September 1980): 69-78. Abridgment of "Walking" in _The City as Dwelling_, 1-7 (Irving, Texas: Center for Civic Leadership, University of Dallas, 1980). Reprinted as "Paradise in Walking," _Resurgence_ 129 (1988): 4-7.

D80c "Silver and the White Earth." _Spring 1980_: 21-48.

D81a "Alchemical Blue and the Unio Mentalis." _Sulfur: A Literary TriQuarterly of the Whole Art_ 1 (1981): 33-50. Reprinted as "Alchemical Blue and the Unio Mentalis" _Spring 54_: 132-148.

D81b "Salt: A Chapter in Alchemical Psychology." In _Images of the Untouched_, edited by Joanne Stroud and Gail Thomas, 111-37 (Dallas: Spring Publications, 1981). Reprinted as "Salt: A Chapter in Alchemical Psychology." In _Salt and the Alchemical Soul_, edited by Stanton Marlan, 145-79 (Woodstock, Conn.: Spring Publications, 1995).

D81c "Silver and the White Earth (Part Two)." _Spring 1981_: 21-66.

D81d "Psicologia Archetipica." Translated by Bianca Garufi. In _Enciclopedia del novecento_, 5: 813-27 (Roma: Istituto dell'Enciclopedia Italiana, 1981). Revised in English as A83b.

D82a "_Anima Mundi_: The Return of the Soul to the World." _Spring 1982_: 71-93. Reprinted with corrections in A92.

D82b "De la certitude mythique." _Cadmos_ 5/17-18, Geneva (1982): 29-51; in English as "On Mythic Certitude," _Sphinx_ 3, London (1990): 224-44.

D83a "The Bad Mother: An Archetypal Approach." _Spring 1983_: 165-81. Reprinted in _Fathers and Mothers_,

2nd edition, edited by Patricia Berry, 102-19 (Dallas: Spring Publications, 1990).

D83b "Yungu Shinrigaku to Toyoshiso." Discussion between James Hillman, Hayao Kawai, and Toshihiko Izutsu. Translated by Mrs. Izutsu. *Shiso* 6/708, Tokyo (1983): 1-35.

D84 "Mars, Arms, Rams, Wars: On the Love of War." In *Nuclear Strategy and the Code of the Warrior: Faces of Mars and Shiva in the Crisis of Human Survival*, edited by R. Grossinger and L. Hough, 247-67 (Berkeley: North Atlantic Books, 1984). Reprinted as "Wars, Arms, Rams, Mars: On the Love of War," in *Facing Apocalypse*, edited by V. Andrews, R. Bosnak, K. W. Goodwin, 118-36 (Dallas: Spring Publications, 1987). And reprinted as "Wars, Arms, Rams, Mars: On the Love of War," in *The Awakened Warrior,* edited by Rick Fields, 70-88 (New York: Tarcher/ Putnam, 1994).

D85a "Extending the Family: From Entrapment to Embrace." The Texas Humanist 7/4 (1985): 6-11. Reprinted in abbreviated form as "Family: From Entrapment to Embrace," *Utne Reader* 27 (1988): 62-65.

D85b "Natural Beauty without Nature." *Spring 1985*: 50-65. An expanded version of a talk delivered at the symposium "Present Tense, Future Perfect?" Collected in the report *LandMark Program*, edited by P. A. Y. Gunter and B. Higgins, 65-69 (Dallas: Landmark Program, 1984).

D85c "The Autonomous Psyche" (with Paul Kugler). *Spring 1985*: 141-61.

D86a "Bachelard's Lautréamont, or Psychoanalysis without a Patient." Afterword essay in Gaston Bachelard, *Lautréamont*, translated by Robert S. Dupree, 103-23 (Dallas: The Dallas Institute Publications, 1986).

D86b "Notes on White Supremacy: Essaying an Archetypal Account of Historical Events." *Spring 1986*: 29-58.

D87a "A Psychology of Transgression Drawn from an Incest Dream: Imagining the Case." *Spring 1987*: 66-76.

D87b "The Dreams of Lost Paradise." *Utne Reader* (January-February 1987): 66-67. Excerpts from F85c.

D88a "Jung's Daimonic Inheritance." *Sphinx* 1, London (1988): 9-19.

D88b "The Right to Remain Silent." *Journal of Humanistic Education and Development* 26/4 (1988): 141-53.

D88c "Sex Talk: Imagining a New Male Sexuality." *Utne Reader* 29 (1988): 76.

D88d "Power and Gemeinschaftsgefühl." *Individual Psychology: The Journal of Adlerian Theory, Research and Practice* 44/1 (1988): 3-12.

D88e "Going Bugs." *Spring 1988*: 40-72.

D88f "Hegel, Giegerich and the U.S.A." *Spring 1988*: 177-80.

D88g "The Animal Kingdom in the Human Dream." *Primavera*, Folio 1 (Fall 1988): no pages. Excerpted from E82.

D88h "Cosmology for Soul: From Universe to Cosmos" (with "Panel Discussions"). In *Cosmos–Life–Religion: Beyond Humanism*, 280-301, 391-409 (Nara: Tenri University Press, 1988). Originally a lecture delivered at the Tenri International Symposium, December 1986. See also D89d and *Ja*89.

D89a "Back to Beyond: On Cosmology" (together with responses). In *Archetypal Process: Self and Divine in Whitehead, Jung, and Hillman*, edited by D. R. Griffin, 213-31, 251-65 (Evanston: Northwestern University Press, 1989).

D89b "And Huge Is Ugly." *Resurgence* 134, Bideford, Devon, England (1989): 4-9. Reprinted in *The Bloomsbury Review* 12/1, Boulder (1992): 3, 20.

D89c "A Course in Miracles: Spiritual Path or Omnipotent Fantasy?" (with Barbara Dunn). *Common Boundary*, Boulder (September-October 1989): 9-12.

D89d "Cosmology for Soul." *Sphinx* 2, London (1989): 17-33. Also see D88h above.

D89e "From Mirror to Window: Curing Psychoanalysis of Its Narcissism." *Spring 1989*: 62-75.

D90a "Plural Art." In *Team Spirit* (exhibition catalogue), 59-65(New York: Independent Curators Inc., 1990).

D90b "The Elephant in *The Garden of Eden*." Paper delivered in honor of the Ernest Hemingway Year, October 1986, at Boise State University, Boise, Idaho. Published in *Spring 50* (1990): 93-115.

D91a "The Practice of Beauty." Lecture delivered at the Museum of Contemporary Art, in Prato, Italy, February 1991. Published in *Sphinx* 4, London (1992): 13-28 and as "The Repression of Beauty" in *Tema Celeste*, International edition 31, Siracusa, Italy (1991): 58-64. Forthcoming in Italian from the Prato Museum.

D91b "City, Sport, and Violence." *Inroads* 7 (1991): 10-18.

D91c "Terrorism in Disguise." *Resurgence* 146, Bideford, Devon, England (1991): 18-19. Extracts from B89.

D92a "One Hundred Years of Solitude, or Can the Soul Ever Get out of Analysis?" In *The Evolution of Psychotherapy: The Second Conference*, edited by Jeffrey Zeig, 313-25; with response to Rollo May, 333-34 (New York: Brunner/Mazel, 1992).

D92b "How Jewish Is Archetypal Psychology?" *Spring 53* (1992): 121-30.

D93a "Concerning the Stone: Alchemical Images of the Goal." *Sphinx* 5, London (1993): 234-265.

D93b "Emotion and Art Therapy." *CREATE: Journal of Creative & Expressive Arts* 3, Toronto (1993): 1-6. Adapted from F92c.

D93c "On the Image." *CREATE: Journal of Creative & Expressive Arts* 3, Toronto (1993): 7-14.

D94a "City, Sport, and Violence." *Psyche and Sports*, edited by Murray Stein and John Hollwitz, 1-16 (Wilmette, Ill.: Chiron Publications, 1994).

D94b "Psychology, Self and Community." *Resurgence* 166, Bideford, devon, England (Sept/Oct: 1994): 18-21.

D94c "Once More Into the Fray–A Response to Wolfgang Giegerich's 'Killings.'" *Spring 56* (1994): 1-18.

D94d "Man is by Nature a Political Animal, Patient as Citizen." In *Speculations after Freud–Psychoanalysis, Philosophy and Culture*, edited by Sonu Shamdasani and Michael Munchow, 27-40 (London: Routledge, 1994).

D94e "The Practice of Beauty." *Archivio* 2, Fiesole [Firenze] (1994): 27-37.

D95a "Pink Madness or Why Does Aphrodite Drive Men Crazy with Pornography?" *Spring 57* (1995): 39-71.

D95b "Neither Nurture nor Nature: Something Else." Early version of Chapter 6 (A96) in *Science and Culture*.

Proceedings of the Institute for Liberal Studies 6 (Frankfort, Kentucky: Kentucky State University, 1995).

D95c *"Pseudologia Fantastica*: A Curious Need to Falsify, Disguise or Destroy the Story of Your Life." *Spring 58* (1995): 83-101. Early version of Chapter 8 (A96).

D96a "Horses and Heroes." *Spring 59* (1996): 125-29.

D96b "Aesthetics and Politics." *Tikkun* 11/6, Oakland (Nov./ Dec. 1996): 38-40.

D96c "Marriage, Intimacy, Freedom." *Spring 60* (1996): 1-11.

D96d "'Psychology–Monotheistic or Polytheistic:' Twenty-five years later." *Spring 60* (1996): 111-25.

E. *Contributions to the* Eranos Jahrbuch

E66 "On Psychological Creativity." In *Eranos Jahrbuch 35-1966*, 349-410 (Zürich: Rhein, 1967). Reprinted in *Art International* 13/7, Lugano (1969). Revised in A72.

E67 "Senex and Puer: An Aspect of the Historical and Psychological Present." In *Eranos Jahrbuch 36-1967*, 301-60 (Zürich: Rhein, 1969). Reprinted in *Art International* 15/1, Lugano (1971). Collected in C79, 3-53.

E68 "The Language of Psychology and the Speech of the Soul." In *Eranos Jahrbuch 37-1968*, 299-356 (Zürich: Rhein, 1970). Also in *Art International* 14/1, Lugano (1970). Revised in A72.

E69 "First Adam, then Eve: Fantasies of Female Inferiority in Changing Consciousness." In *Eranos Jahrbuch 38-1969*, 349-412 (Zürich: Rhein,

       1972). Also in *Art International* 14/7, Lugano (1970). Revised in A72.

E71   "Abandoning the Child." In *Eranos Jahrbuch 40-1971*, 358-406 (Leiden: E. J. Brill,1973). Revised in A75a. Condensed in *Reclaiming the Inner Child*, edited by J. Abrams, 77-86 (Los Angeles: Tarcher, 1990).

E73   "The Dream and the Underworld" In *Eranos Jahrbuch 42-1973*, 91-136 (Leiden: E. J. Brill, 1977). Expanded in A79.

E74   "On the Necessity of Abnormal Psychology." In *Eranos Jahrbuch 43-1974*, 91-135 (Leiden: E. J. Brill, 1977). Reprinted in C80, 1-38.

E75   "Pandaemonium der Bilder: C. G. Jungs Beitrag zum 'Erkenne dich Selbst.'" In *Eranos Jahrbuch 44-1975*, 415-52 (Leiden: E. J. Brill, 1977). Translated by Philipp Wolff into English and included in A83a, D77b.

E76   "Egalitarian Typologies versus the Perception of the Unique." In *Eranos Jahrbuch 45-1976*, 221-80 (Leiden: E. J. Brill, 1980). Reprinted as A86.

E77   "Psychotherapy's Inferiority Complex." In *Eranos Jahrbuch 46-1977*, 121-74 (Frankfurt a/M: Insel Verlag, 1981). Revised in A83a.

E79   "The Thought of the Heart." In *Eranos Jahrbuch 48-1979*, 133-82 (Frankfurt a/M: Insel Verlag, 1981). Reprinted as A84 and in A92.

E81   "The Imagination of Air and the Collapse of Alchemy." In *Eranos Jahrbuch 50-1981*, 273-333 (Frankfurt a/M: Insel Verlag, 1982).

E82   "The Animal Kingdom in the Human Dream." In *Eranos*

Jahrbuch 51-1982, 279-334 (Frankfurt a/M: Insel Verlag, 1983).

E85 "On Paranoia." In *Eranos Jahrbuch 54-1985*, 269-324 (Frankfurt a/M: Insel Verlag, 1987). Reprinted as A88.

E87 "Oedipus Revisited." In *Eranos Jahrbuch 56-1987*, 261-307 (Frankfurt a/M: Insel Verlag, 1989). Reprinted in B91.

E90 "Concerning the Stone: Alchemical Images of the Goal." See D93a, *Ge*E90.

F. Prefaces, Translations, and Occasional Writings

F57 "Editor's Preface" to *The Transcendent Function*, by C. G. Jung, translated by A. R. Pope (privately printed). Zürich: Students' Association of the C. G. Jung Institute, 1957.

F63a "Foreword" (with A. K. Donoghue) to *The Cocaine Papers*, by Sigmund Freud, iii-viii. Vienna / Zürich: Dunquin Press and Spring Publications, 1963.

F63b "Freunde und Feinde." (with Adolf Guggenbühl-Craig). *Schweizer Spiegel* 38, Zürich (1963): 21-26.

F63c "Editor's Introduction" to *The Logos of the Soul*, by Evangelos Christou, i-iv. Vienna / Zürich: Dunquin Press and Spring Publications, 1963 [Reissued; Dallas: Spring Publications, 1987].

F67a "Preface to the American Edition" of *Evil*. Evanston, Ill.: Northwestern University Press, 1967.

F67b   "Preface" to *Satan in the Old Testament*, by Rivkah Scharf Kluger. Evanston, Ill.: Northwestern University Press, 1967.

F67c   "Preface to the American Edition" in *Ancient Incubation and Modern Psychotherapy*, by C. A. Meier. Evanston, Ill.: Northwestern University Press, 1967.

F67d   "De psychologie van het kwaad." *Elseviers Weekblad* 23, Amsterdam (1967): 33-34.

F68   "Editor's Preface to the American Edition" of *Timeless Documents of the Soul*, by S. Hurwitz, M.-L. von Franz, and H. Jacobsohn. Evanston, Ill.: Northwestern University Press, 1968.

F69   "Ein Kampf auf Leben und Tod? Bermerkungen zum Aufstand der Jugend" (with Adolf Guggenbühl-Craig). *Schweizer Spiegel* 44, Zürich (1969): 16-22.

F70a   "An Introductory Note: C. G. Carus–C. G. Jung" in *Psyche (Part One)*, by Carl Gustav Carus. New York / Zürich: Spring Publications, 1970.

F70b   "Preface to the American Edition" of *Conscience*. Evanston, Ill.: Northwestern University Press, 1970.

F70c   Translation from German of "Must Analysis Fail through Its Destructive Aspect?" by Adolf Guggenbühl-Craig. *Spring 1970*: 133-45.

F71   "Avant Propos" to the *Catalogue of Cecil Collins: Recent Paintings*. London: Arthur Tooth and Sons, 1971.

F76   "Publisher's Prefatory Note" to The Visions Seminars, by C. G. Jung. Zürich/New York: Spring Publications, 1976.

F77a "Letter" (on Jung's style compared with T. S. Eliot's). *Journal of Analytical Psychology* 22 (1977): 59.

F77b "Publisher's Preface" to *Hermes and His Children,* by Rafael Lopez–Pedraza, iv (Zürich: Spring Publications, 1977).

F79 "Letter from the Editor for a Tenth Anniversary." *Spring 1979*: i-ii.

F80a "The Children, The Children! An Editorial." *Children's Literature* 8, Storrs, Conn. (1980): 3-6.

F80b "Editor's Preface" to *Facing the Gods* (C80), iv.

F80c "Letter to the Editor" *D Magazine,* Dallas (December 1980): 8.

F80d "Compagnon d'Eranos, communion invisible." In *La Galaxie de l'imaginaire, dérive autour de l'oeuvre de Gilbert Durand,* edited by M. Maffesoli, 217-20 (Paris: Berg International, 1980).

F81a "Entertaining Ideas" *The Institute Newsletter* 1/1 (The Dallas Institute of Humanities and Culture, 1981): 5-7. Reprinted in *Stirrings of Culture*, edited by Robert Sardello and Gail Thomas, 3-5 (Dallas: The Dallas Institute Publications, 1986).

F81b "Letter to Tom Moore" *Corona* 2 (1981): 115-20.

F81c "Vorwort zur 2. Auflage in deutscher Sprache" to *Die Suche nach Innen,* i-ii (Zürich: Daimon Verlag, 1981). See *Ge*A67.

F82a "A Contribution to Soul and Money." In *Soul and Money*, by Russell A. Lockhart, James Hillman et al., 31-43 (Dallas: Spring Publications, 1982). Reprinted in *Money, Food, Drink and Fashion and Analytic Training: Depth Dimensions of Physical Existence* (The Proceedings of the Eighth

International Congress for Analytical Psychology),
edited by John Beebe, 52-59 (Fellbach: Verlag
Adolf Bonz, 1983).

F82b "On Culture and Chronic Disorder." *The Institute
Newsletter* 1/2 (Dallas: The Dallas Institute of Humanities and Culture, 1982): 12-17. Excerpted in
Stirrings of Culture, 15-21.

F82c "City Limits." In *Imagining Dallas*, 55-63 (Dallas: The
Dallas Institute of Humanities and Culture, 1982).

F83a "Interiors in the Design of the City: The Ceiling" *The
Institute Newsletter* 2/1 (Dallas: The Dallas Institute of Humanities and Culture,1983): 11-18.
Reprinted as "Interior and Design of the City:
Ceilings" in *Stirrings of Culture*, 78-84. Excerpt
published as "One Man's Ceiling Is Another
Man's Horror," *Utne Reader* 8 (1985): 104.

F83b "Buffalo's Inner City: A Conversation between Paul
Kugler and James Hillman." *Buffalo Arts Review*
1/1, Buffalo (1983): 1 and 6-7.

F83c "Letter to the Editor" (with Paul Kugler). *Buffalo
Arts Review* 1/2, Buffalo (1983).

F83d Translation from German of "Jottings on the Jung
Film Matter of Heart," by Adolf Guggenbühl-Craig. *Spring 1983*: 199-202.

F84a "Talking as Walking." *The Institute Newsletter* (Dallas: The Dallas Institute of Humanities and
Culture, Fall 1984): 10-12. Reprinted in *Stirrings
of Culture*, 12-14.

F84b "Souls Take Pleasure in Moisture." *The Institute
Newsletter* (Dallas: The Dallas Institute of Humanities and Culture, Fall 1984): 35-38.

Reprinted in *Stirrings of Culture*, 203-05.

F84c "The Spirit of the City" *Buffalo Arts Review* 2/1, Buffalo (1984): 3 and 5.

F85a "The Wildman in the Cage" *Voices: Journal of the American Academy of Psychotherapists* (1985): 30-34. Reprinted as "The Wildman in the Cage: Comment," in *New Men, New Minds: Breaking Male Tradition*, edited by F. Abbott, 182-86 (Freedom, Calif.: Crossing Press, 1987).

F85b "In Memoriam Robert Grinnell." Edited by C. Goodrich (privately printed). Santa Barbara, 1985.

F85c "James Hillman on Animals: A Correspondence with John Stockwell." *Between the Species* 1/2 (1985): 4-8. Excerpted in *Utne Reader* 19 (1987): 66-67.

F85d "Prefazione" to *Trame perdute*, xi-xiii (Milano: Cortina, 1985). See *It*85.

F86a "Selling out to Developers" (Letter to the Editor). *Putnam Observer Patriot*, Putnam, Conn. (9 March 1986): 9.

F86b "Soul and Spirit." In *Carl Jung and Soul Psychology*, edited by E. M. Stern, 29-35 (New York: Haworth Press, 1986). Also in *Voices: The Art and Science of Psychotherapy* 21/3 & 4 (1986): 29-35. Excerpts from A64, 43-47, and A75b, 67-70.

F87a "Bureaucratic Buck Passing" (Letter to the Editor). *Putnam Observer Patriot*, Putnam, Conn. (25 February 1987): 5.

F87b "Behind the Iron Grillwork" (for Clayton Eshleman). *Temblor* 6 (1987): 100.

F88a "Prefazione" to *Saggi sul puer*, xi-xiii (Milano: Cortina, 1988). See *It*88.

F88b "Foreword" to *Inscapes of the Child's World*, by John
        Allan, xiii-xx (Dallas: Spring Publications, 1988).
F89a "Delivering the Male" (Canadian Broadcasting Co. "Ideas,"
        with Robert Bly and Tim Wilson). *Journal of Wild
        Culture*, Toronto (Spring 1989): 6-13.
F89b "La faillite du mouvement spirituel" (Letter). *Guide
        Ressources* 5/1, Montréal (1989): 9.
F90a "Creativity Symposium" (with Bly, Campbell, and
        Pozzo). In *C. G. Jung and the Humanities: Toward
        a Hermeneutics of Culture*, edited by K. Barnaby
        and P. d'Acierno, 153-61 (Princeton: Princeton
        University Press, 1990).
F90b "Jung and Postmodernism–Symposium" (with Casey,
        Kugler, and Miller). In *C. G. Jung and the Humani-
        ties*, 331-40.
F90c "An Education in Psychology. . ." (Address). *Pacifica
        Newsletter* 1/1, Santa Barbara (1990): 3, 9, 12.
F90d "Reply" (to critics of II90b). *LA Weekly*, Los Ange-
        les (June 15-21, 1990): 6.
F90e "Dialogue Continues . . ." (Letter responding to crit-
        ics of D89e). *Common Boundary,* Boulder
        (March-April 1990): 5.
F91a "Reply" (to Ralston's Letter). *The Sun* 188 (1991): 4-5.
F91b "Perché vengono?" Preface to *It*91, vi-ix.
F91c "A Note on 'Soul' in Painting." *Tema Celeste*, Inter-
        national edition 32/33 (1991): 82.
F92a "Two for the Corpse" (Poems). *Exquisite Corpse* 34,
        Baton Rouge (1992): 5.
F92b "Preface: A Memoir from the Author for the 1992
        Edition" of *Re-Visioning Psychology*. See A75b.
F92c "Preface" to *Emotion*. See A60.

F92d "The Heart-Break of America." Concluding Remarks, Multicultural Men's Conference, 25-30 January, 1992, Malibu, Calif. (privately printed, 48).

F92e "Is Therapy the Antithesis of Activism?" *The Phoenix*, Minneapolis (September 1992). Excerpts from B92.

F92f "Some Psalms of Davis" (Four Poems). In *Walking Swiftly: Writings and Images on the Occasion of Robert Bly's 65th Birthday*, edited by Thomas R. Smith, 245-49 (St. Paul, Minn.: Ally Press, 1992).

F92g Excerpts from A83a in *Jungian Literary Criticism*, edited by R. P. Sugg, 129-38 (Evanston, Ill.: Northwestern University Press, 1992).

F92h "J. Hillman on J. Edgar: Food and Fingerprints" (Letter). *Exquisite Corpse* 38, Baton Rouge (1992): 4.

F92i "The Politics of Self-Pity." Excerpts from B92 *Family Therapy Networker* (Nov/Dec 1992): 38-44.

F93a "Preface" to *L'anima del mondo e il pensiero del cuore* (Milano: Garzanti, 1993). See *It*A92.

F93b "Preface to the Brazilian Edition." In *Petrópolis*, edited by Vozes, 1993. See *Po*A64.

F93c "Prefatory Note to the Fifth Printing" of *Archetypal Psychology*. See A83b.

F93d "Substance Abuse and Soul in Things." *Impuls* 2, Oslo (1993): 79-85. (Excerpt from B92.)

F93e "My Hero." *Utne Reader* 57 (1993): 98.

F93f "Letter to the Editor." (re: Katha Pollitt's piece on gender issues.) *Utne Reader* 60 (1993): 11-12.

F94a "Preface to the 1994 edition" and "Postscript—A Critical Review of this Book by the Author." *Insearch* (2nd revised edition of A67). Woodstock, Conn.: Spring Publications, 1994, 3-4, 127-41.

F94b "Psychotherapy and Aesthetic Justice." *Earth Ethics*
      5/2, Washington, D.C. (1994): 6-7 (excerpt from B92).
F94c "The Dark Side of Typing." In *Who am I? Personal-
      ity Types for Self-Discovery,* edited by Robert
      Frager, 112-116 (New York: Putnam's, 1994),
      excerpt from E76.
F95a "Points To Ponder." *Readers Digest* (January 1995): 16.
      (Excerpt from B92.)
F95b "A Psyche the Size of the Earth." In *Ecopsychology,*
      edited by Roszak, Gomes, & Kanner, xvii-xxiii
      (San Francisco: Sierra Club, 1995); and in *Re-
      surgenc*e 168, Bideford, Devon, England (Jan/Feb
      1995): 4-6.; and in *ECOlogic* 26, Oxford, Miss.
      (Summer 1996): 2.
F95c "Let there be dark." Visionfest Remarks, *Utne Reader*
      70 (July/Aug. 1995): 36-37.
F96a "Award Address." New York Open Center. In *Lapis*
      (1996): 7.
F96b "This Question of Images." In *Saga,* edited by Jonathan
      Young, 16-19 (Ashland, Ore.: White Cloud
      Press,1996).
F96c "The President's Analysts." *New Age Journal* (Sept./
      Oct. 1996): 98. By Eden Stone.
F96d "To the Editor of The Day." In *The Day,* New Lon-
      don, Conn. (Nov. 14, 1996): A11.

G. *Unpublished Writings*

G65   "The Courage to Risk Failure." Graduation address
      delivered June 1965 at the American International
      School of Zürich.

G67a "Life and Death in Analysis." Paper delivered at an international conference on suicide, October 1967, San Francisco State University.

G67b "Symbols of Dying." Paper delivered at an international conference on suicide, October 1967, San Francisco State University.

G70 "The Problem of Fantasies and the Fantasy of Problems." Lecture held November 1969 in Brighton. Mimeographed. London: Centre for Spiritual and Psychological Studies, 1970.

G71 "Guidelines for the Future." Lecture held 24 April 1971 in Malvern, England. Mimeographed. London: Centre for Spiritual and Psychological Studies.

G77 "Archetypal Therapy" (with Patricia Berry). Paper presented January 1977 at the "First International Seminar of Archetypal Psychology," Irving, Tex.: University of Dallas.

G79a "Goals for Dallas: Dallas for Goals." Lecture delivered June 1979 to department heads and subheads of the City of Dallas.

G79b "On Graduate Despond." Graduate Dean's opening semester address, September 1979, to the Institute of Philosophic Studies, University of Dallas, Irving, Tex.

G80 "Respect for Air." Contribution to a panel on inspection and maintenance of automobile exhaust emissions, September 1980, Dallas City Hall.

G81 "Imagination Is Bull." Lecture delivered March 1981 at the Dallas Institute of Humanities and Culture.

G83a "Myth and Aging." April 1983, The University of Wisconsin–Milwaukee Center for Twentieth-Century Studies.

G83b   "Academia, the Soul, and the City." December 1983, American Academy of Religion, Annual Meeting, Dallas, Tex.

G83c   "On Dreaming of Pigs: A Jungian View of Interpretation." Lecture delivered November 1983 under the auspices of the Department of English, Yale University, New Haven, Conn.

G87a   "The Open City." Keynote address at "The Soul of Pittsburgh" conference, May 1987, Urban Redevelopment Authority and C. G. Jung Center, Pittsburgh, Penn.

G87b   "Notes on AIDS." October 1987, Dallas Institute of Humanities and Culture, Dallas, Tex.

G88a   "Broken Voices, Healing Voices: Sounding the Deeps" (with Michael McClure and Enrique Pardo). 20 May 1988, San Francisco.

G88b   "The Art of the Soul." Keynote talk at the symposium "Embodying the Spiritual in the Art of the Future," September 1988, San Francisco Art Institute.

G89a   Master of Ceremonies Introduction. Jean Erdman Dance Benefit, 8 June 1989, Marymont Theatre, New York.

G89b   Talk on the Opening Evening. The Shadow in Children's Literature, 17 July 1989, Simmons College, Boston.

G90a   "Figuring the Future." In honor of C. West Churchman, Systems Philosophy Conference, July 1990, Portland, Ore.

G90b   "Jane Pratt: In Memoriam." August 1990, Bridgewater, Conn.

G90c   "Anthropos Phusei Politikon Zoon (Man Is by Nature a Political Animal) or Patient as Citizen." Lecture delivered October 1990 at the Freud Museum Conference "Speculations," London.

G90d "Your Emotions Are Not Yours: Arts Therapy and the Handicapped." Keynote address, "La Sapienza," University of Rome Conference, 7 November 1990, Roma. Partly included in F92c.

G91 "Soul and Beauty in Today's Urban World." Keynote lecture, Konan University, 40th anniversary symposium "Man and Soul in Modern Times," December 1991, Kobe, Japan.

G92 "Lustful Images: A Necessary Defense of Pornography." Welcoming address, Festival of Archetypal Psychology, 7 July 1992, University of Notre Dame, Notre Dame, Ind.

G94a "Geography at the End of History." Lecture, October 1994, Moorhead State University, Moorhead, Minn.

G94b "Mind, Memory, Narrative." Lecture, October 1994, Montana State University, Bozeman, Mont.

G94c "In the Garden: A Psychological Memoir." For *Festschrift* in honor of Toshihiko Izutsu, 1994.

G95a "Aging." Lecture, sponsored by C. G. Jung Society, April 1995, St. Louis.

G95b "The Seduction of Black." (Extended version of *It*95b.)

G95c "Memorial Reading for Etheridge Knight." November 1995, Teachers and Writers Collaborative, New York.

G95d "Case History–Evolution or Revelation." Address, *Evolution of Psychotherapy* Conference, December 1995, Erickson Foundation, Las Vegas.

G95e "The Segregation of Beauty." Lecture, December 1995, Ninth Annual Meeting, International Skye, New York.

G95f "Architecture, City, Soul." Talk, December 1995, Conference on City Planning, Trento, Italia.

G96a "Can there be Ethics without Aesthetics?–Aesthetic Response as Political Action." Talk at *Tikkun* Summit for Ethics and Meaning, April 1996, Washington, D.C.

G96b "Nature, City, Soul." Talk on the occasion of *Citizen of Chiavari Award*. Chiavari, Italia. April 1996

G96c "Psychology–Monotheistic or Polytheistic: Twenty-Five Years Later." Lecture, April 1996, Casa Machiavelli, Firenze. See D96d.

G96d "Hermetic Intoxication." Address, May 1996, University of Torino.

G96e "Milennial Psychology." Public Lecture, May 1996, Banco Popolare Commercio, Milano.

G96f "Hera, Goddess of Marriage." Public Lecture, February 1996, Santa Barbara [Revised from similar lectures, Omaha. October 1994, and Berkeley, June 1994].

G96g Interview on the Language of Therapy, with Joe Coppin, February 1996, Auburn, Calif.

G96h "The Natural, the Literal, and the Real." Talk at the conference, *The Challenge of Realism*, June 1996, Newington-Cropsey Foundation, New York.

G96i *The Soul's Code.* 5 Questions answered for Oprah Online. (Nov. 15, 1996). By Michael Cook.

H. Interviews

H68 "A Psychologist Talks about . . ." (Interview by Kenneth L. Wilson). *Christian Herald* 91 (1968): 22-28, 54-58.

H83a "Jungian Psychology and Oriental Thought" (with Toshihiko Izutsu and Hayao Kawai). Translated into Japanese by Mrs. Izutsu. *Shiso* 8/708 (1983): 1-35.

H83b "Let the Creatures Be" (Interview by Thomas Moore). *Parabola: Myth and Quest for Meaning* 8/2 (1983): 49-54.

H84 "Une psychologie archétypale, entretien James Hillman/Michel Cazenave." In *Carl G. Jung,* Cahier de l'Herne 46, 491-99 (Paris: l'Herne, 1984).

H86a "Dialogue with James Hillman" (by Shaun McNiff). *Art Therapy* 3/3 (1986): 99-110.

H86b "Part One of a Discussion on Psychology and Poetry" (by Clayton Eshleman). *Sulfur: A Literary Tri-Quarterly of the Whole Art* 6/1 (1986): 56-74. Reprinted as "A Discussion with James Hillman on Psychology and Poetry," in *Antiphonal Swing* by Clayton Eshleman, 205-16 (New York: McPherson, 1989).

H86c "Il nemico numero uno? L'Aspirina" (Interview by Silvia Lagorio). *L'Unita*, Roma edizione, 10 December 1986.

H87 "Conversation with James Hillman." In *The Search for Omm Sety*, by Jonathan Cott, 221-25 (New York: Doubleday, 1987).

H88a "James Hillman on Soul and Spirit: An Interview by Barbara Dunn." *Common Boundary* 6/4, Boulder (1988): 5-11.

H88b "Spezziamo quel lettino: Hillman risponde ai suoi critici" (Interview by Caterina Cardona). *L'Espresso*, 4 December 1988, 192-97.

H88c   "Imagination in Education" (Interview by Brian Nicholson). Dartington Hall, Bideford, Devon, England, November 1988.

H89a   "Conversation avec James Hillman" (Interview by Ginette Paris). _Guide Ressources_ 4/3, Montréal (1989): 50-56.

H89b   "The Erotics of Publishing" (Interview by Clarissa Pinkola Estes). _The Bloomsbury Review_ 9/5, Boulder (1989): 6-7.

H89c   "Therapy and Society" (Interview by Michael Ventura). _LA Weekly_, 1989. First part reprinted in _Men's Council Journal_ 7 (1990): 6-8, 16. Expanded in B92.

H89d   "L'Anima del Mondo" (Interview by Silvia Lagorio). _L'Unita_, Milano edizione, 6 December 1989.

H90   "The Myth of Therapy" (Interview by Andrew Dick). _East–West_ (February 1990): 68-72.

H90b   "Could Psychology Be Part of the Disease, not Part of the Cure?" (Conversation with Michael Ventura). _LA Weekly_ 12/26 (1990): 16-25. Reprinted in _Men's Council Journal_ 7 (1990).

H90c   "Venti di guerra" (Interview by Claudio Risé). _Vanity Fair (Italia)_ (November 1990): 238-42.

H91a   "The Myth of Therapy" (Interview by Sy Safransky). _The Sun 185_ (1991). Excerpted in _Utne Reader_ 49 (1992): 98-99. Reprinted in "Is Psychotherapy a Waste of Time?" _Yoga Journal_ 104 (1992): 52-54, 56, 110.

H91b   "Hillman on Sense of Community" (Interview by Forrest Craver). _Wingspan_ (Oct-Dec 1991): 10-12. Excerpted in _In Context_ 30 (1991): 20. Reprinted in full in _Edges_ 4/2, Toronto (1991):

23-26, 36, and in *Wingspan: Inside the Men's Movement*, edited by Christopher Harding, 242-48 (New York: St. Martin's Press, 1992).

H91c "Intervista a James Hillman su Wallace Stevens" (by Vittorio Lingiardi). *Poesia* 4/36, Milano (1991): 10-11.

H91d "Nel regno di Marte" (Interview by Maria Nadotti). *Linea d'Ombra 59*, Milano (1991): 17-19.

H92a "Interview" (by Suzanne Ramljak). *Sculpture* (March-April 1992): 14-17.

H92b "Knocking Psychotherapy" (Interview by Bruce McCabe). *Boston Globe*, 27 July 1992, 30-34.

H92c "We've Had a Thousand Years of Love, and the World's Getting Worse" (Conversation with Michael Ventura). *LA Weekly* (May 22-28, 1992).

H93a "Youth and the Yearning for Myth" (with Michael Meade). By Vaughan Hawthorne. *Kindred Spirit* 2/11. Totnes, Devon, England.

H93b "Making Connections (what older people have to offer the young)." By Emma Coyle. *Vantage* (Nov-Dec 1993). Cade Communications: Chicago, Ill.

H93c "Hvalfangst, teknologi og psykologisk aktivisme." By Espen Stoknes. *Impuls* 4 (1993). Psykologis–institutt, Oslo.

H94a "Animal Presence." In *Talking on the Water,* edited by Jonathan White, 121-35 (San Francisco: Sierra Club, 1994).

H94b "Arianna's Virtual Candidate." By Maureen Orth. In *Vanity Fair* (Nov. 1994): 198/col. 3.

H94c "100 Years–The Elders Remember." By Ulfried Geuter (Sept. 29, 1994). Transcript of a German Radio Program.

H95a "How the Soul is Sold" (Interview by Emily Yoffe). *New York Times Magazine* (April 23, 1995): 44-49.

H95b "The Soul of the Matter" (Interview by Wes Nisker). *Inquiring Mind* 11/2 (1995): 8-10.

H95c "When you're Healed, Send me a Postcard" (Interview by Suzi Gablik). *Conversations Before the End of Time* (1995): 176-201. New York: Thames and Hudson.

H95d "Profile" (Interview by Jon Spayde in "100 Visionaries") *Utne Reader* 67 (1995): 67.

H95e "Wer immer nur über die Kindheit spricht, entpolitisiert" (Interview by Ulfried Geuter). *Psychologie Heute,* Weinheim (Jan. 95): 46-49.

H96a "La Nostra Anima? Ha un Profondo Bisogno di Bellezza" (Interview by Christina Guarinelli). *Marie Claire,* Milano (July 1996): 61-64.

H96b "Umani Disagi di Città Anoressiche." (Interview by Elisabetta Confaloni). *Il manifesto* (April 19, 1994): 28.

H96c "Waking Up with the House on Fire" (Interview by Steve Perry). *City Pages,* Minneapolis (Oct. 2, 1996): 16-20, 22.

H96d "Soul Man" (Interview by Sean Abbott). *At Random* No. 15, New York (Fall 1996): 60-65.

H96e "Soul Man" (Interview by Eddie Silva). *The Riverfront Times,* St. Louis (Oct. 2-8, 1996): 29-30.

H96f "Star of The Week" feature under Oprah's Community, Oprah Online. (Nov. 15, 1996). Interviewed by Elizabeth Porter.

H96g "James Hillman says, it's NOT all in your head" (Interview by Stephen Capen). *Shambala Sun,* Boulder (Nov. 1996): 20-25.

Translations of A-H
and First Publications in Foreign Languages

Nota bene: The first two letters of the codes in this section refer to the language into which the work has been translated. The remaining characters identify the work in its original form (from sections A through H). If the translation is a collection of various works, the code will be only the language and date of publication. These collections are found at the ends of language sections.

Czech

*Cz*A64   *Dose a Sebevrazda.* Translated by Ludvik Fojtik. Praha: Sagittarius, 1997.

Danish

*Da*A64   *Selvmord og sjaelelig forvandling.* Translated by Dita Mendel (Afterword by Eigil Nyborg). Copenhagen: Rhodos, 1978.

Dutch

*Du*A67   *Zelfonderzoek.* Translated by Frits Lancel. Rotterdam: Lemniscaat, 1969.

*Du*A75a *Verraad en verlangen: beelden uit de archetypische psychologie* (only Parts 1-5). Translated by Els Pikaar. Rotterdam: Lemniscaat, 1984. See also F67d.

French

FrA64   "A la Rencontre du Risque de Suicide." (only Chapter
        5). Traduction par Claude Lagedec, *Frontières* (2
        parts) 3/1, Montréal (1990): 27-46; 3/2 (1990): 31-35.

FrE67   "Kronos-Senex et Puer." Traduction par Monique
        Salzmann, *Cahiers de psychologie jungienne* 18
        (1978): 36-55.

FrA72   *Le mythe de la psychanalyse.* Traduction par Philippe
        Mikriammos. Paris: Imago, 1977. Also, excerpts from
        Part III in "Le retour de Dionysos dans la conscience,"
        Art et thérapie 32/33, Blois (1989): 90-98.

FrB72   *Pan et le cauchemar.* Traduction par Th. Auzas, Marie-
        Jeanne Benmussa, et Monique Salzmann. Paris:
        Imago, 1979.

FrD73a "Anima." This includes D74a. Traduction par Viviane
        Thibaudier. In *Animus et Anima* (with Emma
        Jung), 109-221(Paris: Seghers, 1981).

FrF77b "Préface" to *Hermès et ses enfants dans la psychothérapie,*
        par Rafael Lopez–Pedraza. Traduction par Marie-
        Jeanne Benmussa et Th. Auzas. Paris: Imago, 1980.

Fr82   *Le polythéisme de l'âme.* Traduction par Thomas
        Johnson. Paris: Mercure de France-Le Mail, 1982.
        Includes C80, 1-38, D76a, and the expanded version
        of D71a published in *The New Polytheism.*

FrF82b "La culture et la chronicité du désordre." Traduction
        par Michele-Isis Brouillet, *La petite revue de
        philosophie* 9/2 (1988): 11-25.

FrB85   *La cuisine de Freud* (avec Charles Boer). Traduction
        par Anne Ledoux-Mabille et Micheline Drain. Paris:
        Payot, 1985.

*Fr*B89   *La beauté de psyché:L'âme et ses symboles.* Préface par
          Ginette Paris. Montréal: Le Jour-Sogides 1993.

*Fr*D89e   "L'Âme et le jardin" (only 71-75). Traduction par
          Paul Carle, *Quatretemps*, Bull. Soc. d'animation du
          Jardin et l'Institute de Montréal, 14/4 (1990): 14-17.

*Fr*D89e   "Du miroir à la fenêtre: Guérir la psychanalyse de
          son narcissisme." Traduction par Antoine Pinterovic,
          Hérésies 5, Bruxelles (1994): 29-46.

*Fr*H89c   "La Thérapie serait-elle une maladie?" Traduction et
          adaptation par Michel Saint-Germain/Bellefeuille,
          Guide Ressources 7/2, Montréal (1991): 14-23.

*Fr*B92   (___) Paris: Fleurs Essences et Harmonie. (Forth-
          coming.)
          See also D80a, D82b, F80d, F89b, H84, H89a.

German

*Ge*A64   *Selbstmord und seelische Wandlung.* Translated by
          Hilde Binswanger. Foreword by Adolf
          Guggenbühl-Craig. Zürich: Rascher Verlag, 1966.
          Zürich: Schweizer Spiegel Verlag, 1979.

*Ge*D64   "Verrat." Translated by Wolfgang Giegerich and Ruth
          Horine, *Analytische Psychologie* 10 (1979): 81-
          102.

*Ge*A67   *Die Begegnung mit sich Selbst.* Translated by
          Marianne von Eckhardt-Jaffé. Stuttgart: Klett
          Verlag, 1969. 2nd edition, with a new foreword,
          under the title *Die Suche nach Innen: Psychologie
          und Religion.* Zürich: Daimon Verlag, 1981.

*Ge*D70c "Über das Senex Bewusstsein." Translated by Giesel
          Henney, Stuttgart, *Gorgo* 3 (1980): 23-42.

*Ge*B71 "Das Gefühl und die Fühlfunktion." In *Zur Typologie C. G. Jungs* (with Marie-Louise von Franz), 105-214 (Fellbach: Verlag Adolf Bonz, 1980).

*Ge*D71a "Die Psychologie: Monotheistisch oder polytheistisch?" Translated by Gudula Herrmann, *Gorgo* 1, Stuttgart (1979): 1-21.

*Ge*B72 *Pan und die natürliche Angst-über die Notwendigkeit der Alpträume für die Seele.* Translated by Trude Fein. Zürich: Raben Reihe, Schweizer Spiegel Verlag, 1981.

*Ge*D73a "Anima." Translated by Hildegard Theus, *Gorgo* 5, Stuttgart (1981): 45-81.

*Ge*D74a "Anima II." Translated by Gert Quenzer, *Gorgo* 6, Stuttgart (1981): 56-89.

*Ge*A79 *Am Anfang war das Bild: Unsere Träume-Brucke der Seele zu den Mythen.* Translated by Doris Engelke. Munich: Kösel, 1983.

*Ge*F82a "Seele und Geld." Translated by Wolfgang Giegerich, *Gorgo* 4, Stuttgart (1980): 31-40.

*Ge*A83a *Die Heilung erfinden: Eine psychotherapeutische Poetik.* Translated by Kathi Staufer-Zahner. Zürich: Raben Reihe, Schweizer Spiegel Verlag, 1986. An excerpt from Part III was published as "Was will die Seele?" *Analytische Psychologie* 17 (1986): 160-85.

*Ge*D84 "Die Welt des Mars. Über die Liebe zum Krieg und im Krieg." Translated by Wolfgang Giegerich, *Gorgo* 15, Stuttgart (1988): 29-46.

*Ge*B85 *Sigmund Freud: Mein Kochbuch* (with Charles Boer). Translated by Doris Engelke. Frankfurt a/M: Eichborn Verlag, 1986.

*Ge*D85c "Die autonome Psyche" (with Paul Kugler). Translated by Wolfgang Giegerich. *Gorgo* 10, Stuttgart (1986): 3-23.

*Ge*H86a "Dialog mit James Hillman." Translated and abridged by Bettina Egger, *Forum fur Kunsttherapie* 2/2, Bern (1989): 32-37.

*Ge*D87a "Eine Psychologie der Überschreitung: gewonnen aus einem Inzesttraum." *Gorgo* 13, Stuttgart (1987): 27-39.

*Ge*D89e "Vom Spiegel zum Fenster; den Narzissmus der Psychanalyse heilen." *Gorgo* 16, Stuttgart (1989): 5-18 (together with excerpts of interviews from the Italian press and responses by A. Guggenbühl-Craig, N. Micklem, and M. Jacoby, 19-34).

*Ge*B92 *Hundert Jahre Psychotherapie und der Welt Geht's immer schlechter.* Translated by Clemens Wilhelm. Solothurn / Düsseldorf: Walter, 1993.

*Ge*E90 "Über den Stein–Bilder vom alchemistischem Ziel." In *Auferstehung und Unsterblichkeit,* translated by Susanne Schreiner, Eranos New Series 1, 53-83 (München: Wilhelm Fink, 1993).

*Ge*D91a "Die Kraft der Schönheit." *Der Zeitpunkt* 11/12, Bellach, Switzerland (Sep-Dez: 1993): 6-13.

See also D63, E75, F63b, F69, F81c, G92c.

Hungarian

*Hu*A64 "A Halálélmény" (only Chapter 4). Translated by Gyula Kodolçnyi, *Magyar Szemle* ll/l (1993): 48-62.

Italian

*It*F63c "Editor's Preface" to *Il logos dell'anima*, by Evangelos Christou. Translated by Emilio di Domenico. Roma: Città Nuova, 1987.

*It*A64 *Il suicidio e l'anima*. Translated by Aldo Giuliani. Roma: Astrolabio, 1972.

*It*D64 "Il tradimento." *Rivista di psicologia analitica* 2/1 (1971): 177-98. Also in *It*E67.

*It*D66 "Modello archetipico di inibizione alla masturbazione." In *Problemi di psicologia analitica: una antologia postjunghiana*, edited by Luigi Zoja, 80-98 (Napoli: Liguori, 1983).

*It*A67 "Vita interiore: l'inconscio come esperienza" (only Chapter 3). *Rivista di psicologia analitica* 4/1 (1973): 67-98.

*It*B67 "Commento psicologico." In *Kundalini*, by Gopi Krishna, translated by Paolo Colombo (Roma: Astrolabio, 1971).

*It*E67 *Senex et Puer, e il tradimento*. Translated by Matelda Giuliani Talarico. Padua/Venezia: Marsilio, 1973 [reprinted; 1990]. See also *It*D64.

*It*E68 "Linguaggio della psicologia e linguaggio dell'anima." *Rivista di psicologia analitica* 3/2 (1972): 308-74.

*It*D70d "Psicologia archetipica." Translated by Paola Donfrancesco and Roberto Tamarri, edited by Bianca Garufi, *L'immaginale* 6, Lecce (1987): 23-59.

*It*D71a "Psicologia: monoteistica o politeistica." In *Il nuovo politeismo* (with David Miller), translated by Mauro Bonacci and Paola Donfrancesco, edited by Bianca Garufi, 115-54(Milano: Comunità, 1983).

ItA72   *Il mito dell'analisi.* Translated by Aldo Giuliani. Milano: Adelphi, 1979 [new edition; 1991].

ItB72   *Saggio su Pan.* Translated by Aldo Giuliani. Milano: Adelphi, 1979.

ItD72b "Analisi e fallimento." *Rivista di psicologia analitica* 3/1 (1972): 211-19.

ItD73a "Anima" (first part). *Rivista di psicologia analitica* 21 (1980).

ItD74a "Anima" (second part). Translated by Luciana and Gianni Baldaccini, *Rivista di psicologia analitica* 27 (1983): 101-40.

ItD74c "C. G. Jung e la teoria archetipica." In *Problemi di psicologia analitica*, 50-79. Also in ItD66.

ItD74d "Pothos, la nostalgia del puer aeternus." Translated by Francesco and Paola Donfrancesco, *Prassi e teoria* 4 (1980): 123-36. Also in *Saggi sul puer*, edited by Francesco Donfranceso and Bianca Garufi (Milano: Cortina, 1988).

ItE74   "Ananke e Atena: La necessita della psicologia anormale." In *La vana fuga dagli dei*, translated by Adriana Bottini (Milano: Adelphi, 1991). See ItA88.

ItA75b *Re-visione della psicologia.* Translated by Aldo Giuliani. Milano: Adelphi, 1983.

ItD76b "Un primo sfondo al pensiero di Jung." Translated by Franca Cassuto, *L'immaginale* 4, Lecce (1985): 21-33.

ItD76c "Carl Gustav Jung ed Helene Preiswerk." *Anima* 2/2, Firenze (1994): 128-139.

ItD77a "Ricerche sull'immagine" (first part). Translated by Ada Bianchi Maffei, *Rivista di psicologia analitica* 20 (1979): 31-63.

*It*D77b "Il pandemonio delle immagini. Il contributo di Jung al 'conosci te stesso.'" Translated by Paola Donfrancesco, *Testimonianze* 23, Firenze (1980): 61-90. See E75.

*It*D78c "Il valore terapeutico del linguaggio alchemico." *Rivista di psicologia analitica* 17 (1978): 143-61.

*It*A79 *Il sogno e il mondo infero.* Translated by Paola Donfrancesco and edited by Bianca Garufi. Milano: Comunità, 1984 [reprinted; Milano: Mondadori-ll Saggiatore, 1988, 1996].

*It*D80a "La misura degli eventi." Translated by Francesco Donfrancesco, *Anima* 2 (1989): 114-26.

*It*D81a "Blu alchemico e unio mentalis." Translated by Milka Ventura and Veronica Park, edited by Bianca Garufi, *L'immaginale* 7, Lecce (1986): 33-46.

*It*D81b "Il Sale: un capitolo di psicologia alchimistica." Translated by Sergio Rinaldelli, *Hellas: rivista di letteratura sul mito* 8/9 (1985): 67-86. Published also as "Sale: un capitolo della psicologia alchemica," in *L'Intatta*, translated by Marta Cohen Hemsi, 132-64 (Como: RED, 1987).

*It*D82a "Anima mundi, il ritorno dell'anima al mondo." Translated by Paola Donfrancesco, *Testimoruanze* 24, Firenze (1981): 123-40. Reprinted in *L'immaginale* 5, Lecce (1985): 5-25, and in *It*A92.

*It*D82b "Della certezza mitica." *L'immaginale* 6, Lecce (1986): 63-80. First published in *Fr*82.

*It*A83a *Le storie che curano.* Translated by Milka Ventura and Paola Donfrancesco. Edited by Francesco Donfrancesco and Bianca Garufi. Milano: Cortina, 1984.

ItB83   *Intervista su amore, anima e psiche* (with Marina Beer). Bari: Laterza, 1983. Expanded in B83. Chapter 9 of B83 is published as "Sul mio scrivere," translated by Maria Rosario Buri, *L'immaginale* 2, Lecce (1984): 5-17.

It85   *Trame perdute.* Translated by many and edited by Francesco Donfrancesco and Bianca Garufi. Milano: Cortina, 1985. Selections from A75a and also containing B71, D70b, D75b, D83a, F82b.

ItA85   *Anima: anatomia di una nozione personificata.* Translated by Adriana Bottini. Milano: Adelphi, 1989.

ItB85   *La cucina del dottor Freud* (with Charles Boer). Translated by Pierre Denivelle (a.k.a. Vittorio Serra Boccara). Milano: Cortina, 1986.

ItD86b   "Sulla supremazia del bianco." Translated by Beatrice Rebecchi Cecconi, edited by Bianca Garufi, *L'immaginale* 10, Lecce (1988): 5-35. "La supremazia del bianco." Translated by Paola Donfrancesco, *Anima* 5, Firenze (1991): 93-111; part two in *Anima* 6, Firenze (1992): 92-111.

ItD87a   "Da un sogno d'incesto: una psicologia della trasgressione." Translated by Paola Donfrancesco, *Anima* 4, Firenze (1990): 24-38. Reprinted in *Trappole seduttive,* edited by Maria Irmgard Wuehl, 111-127 (Milano: Vivarium, 1996).

ItD87c   "Il demoniaco come eredita di Jung." In *Presenze ed eredità culturale di C. G. Jung,* edited by L. Zoja, 93-102 (Milano: Cortina, 1987).

ItD87d   "Del diritto a non parlare." Translated by Beatrice Rebecchi Cecconi, edited by Bianca Garufi, *L'immaginale* 9, Lecce (1987): 19-33.

*It*88   *Saggi sul puer.* Translated by Paola Donfrancesco, Milka
Ventura, and Silvia Lagorio. Edited by Francesco
Donfrancesco and Bianca Garufi. Milano:
Cortina, 1988. Includes D73c, D74d, D76a,
D79b, D79c, F88a.

*It*A88   "Sulla paranoia." Translated by Adriana Bottini, in
La Vana fuga dagli dei [together with *It*E74]
(Milano: Adelphi, 1991).

*It*D88a   "L'Eredità demonica di Jung." Translated by Paola
Donfrancesco, *Anima* 2/4, Firenze (1996): 129-136.

*It*D88d   "Potere e sentimento sociale." In *General Aspects of
the Analytic Process* (Torino: Saiga, 1990).

*It*D88h   "Una cosmologia per l'anima. Al di la dell'umanismo."
Translated by Beatrice Rebecchi Cecconi and edited
by Bianca Garufi, *Aut aut,* Milano / Firenze (1989):
270-84.

*It*B89a   "Sul sogno" [Chapter 10 only, less the prefatory note].
No translator listed, edited by M. T. Colonna and
Bianca Garufi, *Rivista di psicologia analitica* 43
(1989): 71-94.

*It*D89b   ". . . ed enorme é brutto." Translated by Paola
Donfrancesco, with illustrated letters by Mimmo
Paladino, *Tema Celeste* 37-38 (Autumn 1992): 42-
47.

*It*B89c   *Fuochi blu.* Translated by Adriana Bottini. Milano:
Adelphi. 1996.

*It*D89e   "Dal narcisismo alla finestra . . ." No translator listed. In
Itinerari del pensiero junghiano, edited by Paolo
Aite and Aldo Carotenuto, (Milano: Cortina,
1989). Excerpts also in "Oltre il giardino," *Epoca*
13 (1988): 170-75.

*It*B90 "Edipo rivisitato." Translated by Alessandro Serra, in *Variazioni su Edipo* (with K. Kerényi), 73-143 (Milano: Cortina, 1992).

*It*91 *Animali del sogno*. Translated by Alessandro Serra and David Verzoni. Milano: Cortina, 1991. Contains an original preface (F91b) and D88e, D90a, E82.

*It*A92 *L'anima del mondo e il pensiero del cuore*. Translated by Paola Donfrancesco. Milano: Garzanti, 1993. Includes also D73d and F93a.

*It*B92 *100 anni di psicoterapia e il mondo va sempre peggio*. Translated by Paola Donfrancesco. Milano: Garzanti, 1993.

*It*D92 "Emozione, immagine, simbolo." Translated by Clotilde Calabi, in *Estetica 1992: Forme del simbolo*, edited by S. Zecchi, 67-91 (Bologna: il Mulino, 1992).

*It*93a "Le nostre emozioni non sono nostre." Translated by Paola Donfrancesco, *Anima* 2/1, Firenze (1993): 15-25. (Partially adapted from F92c.)

*It*93b "Prefazione: esilo, nostalgia e bellezza." Translated by Paola Donfrancesco, in *Memorie di Luce* by Francesco Donfrancesco, 7-12 (Firenze: Ponte Alle Grazie, 1993).

*It*D94e "La repressione della bellezza." *Archivio* 2, Fiesole (1994): 37-48.

*It*95a "Psicoterapia: civilizzazione o cultura?" Translated by Paola Donfrancesco, *Anima* 2/3, Firenze (1995): 8-19.

*It*95b "Il colore 'non-colore.'" In *I colori della vita,* edited by P. Bianucci, 19-26 (Torino: La Stampa, 1995).

*It*96   *Oltre l'umanismo.* Translated by Paola Donfrancesco.
          Bergamo: Moretti & Vitali, 1996. (Contains D89a,
          D82b, D88h, D89e, D70d.)
*It*A96   *Forme del Potere.* Translated by Paola Donfrancesco.
          Milano: Garzanti, 1996.
*It*G96d   "Ermes domina il mondo." Commentary by Luigi
          Zoja, Milano: *Il Sole–24 Ore* 170 (June 23, 1996):
          28.
See also D73d, D81d, D91a, F85d, F88a, F91b, F93a, H86c,
          H88b, H89d, H90c, H91c, H91d.

Japanese

*Ja*A64   *Jisatsu to Tamashii.* Translated by Kazuhiko Higuchi.
          Osaka: Sogensha, 1982.
*Ja*A67   *Niteki Sekai e no Tankyu.* Translated by Kazuhiko
          Higuchi. Osaka: Sogensha, 1990.
*Ja*A79   (*The Dream and the Underworld*). Osaka: Sogensha.
          (Forthcoming).
*Ja*A83b   (*Archetypal Psychology*). Osaka: Sogensha.
*Ja*D76a   As an Appendix in *Ja*83b.
*Ja*D83a   "Warui Hahaoya, Yoi Kodomo" (Bad Mother, Good
          Child). Translated by Tsuneko Matsuo, in *Oya
          to Ko No Kizuna* (Parents-Child Bonding), ed-
          ited by Kawai, Kobayashi, and Nakane, 256-76
          (Osaka: Sogensha, 1984).
*Ja*A85   (*Anima: An Anatomy of a Personified Notion*). Osaka:
          Sogensha. (Forthcoming).
*Ja*B85   *Furoito no Ryori Dokuhon.* Translated by Sadamu
          Kimura and Yoshiaki Ikekura. Tokyo: Seidosha,
          1991.

*Ja*89 "Tamashii no kusumologii." In *Kosumosu-seimei-shukyo* (Nara: Tenri University Press, 1989). See D88h and D89d.
See also D83b, D88h, G91, H83a.

Polish

*Pl*A64 *Samobójstwo A Przemiana Psychiczna*. Translated by Dariusz Rogalski. Warszawa: Wydawnictwo KR, 1996.

Portuguese

*Po*A64 (*Suicide and the Soul*). Petrópolis: Vozes. (Forthcoming).

*Po*A67 *Una Busca interior em psicologia e religião*. Translated by Aracéli Martins and José Joaquim Sobral. São Paulo: Editora Paulinas, 1985.

*Po*B67 "Comentçrios Psicológicos" to *Kundalini*, by Gopi Krishna, translated by Ernesto Bono (Rio de Janeiro: Editora Record, n.d.).

*Po*B71 "A Funcao Sentimento." Translated by Adail Ubirajara Sobral with technical revision by Lucia Rosenberg and Gustavo Barcellos, in *A Tipologia de Jung* (São Paulo: Editora Cultrix, 1990).

*Po*A72 *O Mito da Análise*. Translated by Norma Telles. Rio de Janeiro: Editora Paz e Terra, 1984.

*Po*D73c "A Grande Mae, seu Filho, seu Heroi, e O Puer." Translated by Pedro Penteado Kujawski, in *Pais e Maes*, 97-153 (São Paulo: Símbolo, 1979).

*Po*A75a *Estudos de Psicológia Arquetipica.* Translated by Pedro
          Ratis e Silva. Rio de Janeiro: Achiamé, 1981.

*Po*D76a "Picos e Vales." Translated by Adelaide Petters
          Lessa, in *No Caminho de Autoconhecimento*, 91-
          118 (São Paulo: Editora Pioneira, 1982).

*Po*C80   *Encarando os Deuses.* Translated by Claudio
          Giordana. São Paulo: Cultrix/Pensamento, n.d.

*Po*A83b *Psicológia Arquetipica.* Translated by Lucia
          Rosenberg and Gustavo Barcellos. São Paulo:
          Editora Cultrix, 1991.

*Po*B83   *Entre vistas: conversas com Laura Pozzo sobre*
          psicoterapia, biografia, amor, alma, sonhos,
          trabalho, imaginacao e o estado da cultura.
          Translated by Lucia Rosenberg and Gustavo
          Barcellos. São Paulo: Editora Summus, 1989.

*Po*A85   *Anima: Anatomia de uma Nocao Personificada.* Trans-
          lated by Lucia Rosenberg and Gustavo Barcellos.
          São Paulo: Editora Cultrix, 1990.

*Po*B85   *O Livro de Cozhina do Dr. Freud* (with Charles Boer).
          Translated by Silvio Cancellotti. São Paulo:
          Editora Paz e Terra, 1986.

*Po*B91   *Édipo e Variações.* Translated by Gustavo Barcellos.
          Petrópolis: Vozes, 1995.

*Po*B92   *Cem anos de psicoterapia... e o mundo está cada vez*
          pior. Translated by Norma Telles. São Paulo:
          Summus Editorial , 1995.

*Po*93   *Cidade e Alma.* Edited and translated by Lucia
          Rosenberg and Gustavo Barcellos. São Paulo:
          Editora Studio Nobel, (Forthcoming). Includes
          D78a, D79d, D80b, D82a, D84, D85b, D89b,
          D91b, F82a, F82b,F83a, G90c. See also F93b.

Russian

*Ru*A83a *Isezeliajuschij Viemysel.* Translated by J. Donetz, V. Zelensky. St. Petersburg: BSK Publ. Co., 1996.
*Ru*A83b *Archetipicheskaya psichologia.* Translated by J. Donetz, V. Zelensky. St. Petersburg: BSK Publ. Co., 1996.

Spanish

*Sp*F77b "Prefacio a la Edición en Lengua Hispánica" to *Hermes y sus Hijos*, by Rafael Lopez–Pedraza, translated by Carlos Valbuena (Caracas: Editorial Ateneo, 1980).
*Sp*B92 *Cien años de psicoanálisis. . . y todo sigue igual.* Translated by Jaime Collyer. Buenos Aires: Editorial Sudamericana, 1995.
*Sp*94 *La Cultura y el Alma Animal.* Translated by Maria J. Bustamante. Caracas: Fundacion Polar, 1994.
*Sp*E73 "El Sueño y el Inframundo." In *Arquetipos y Símbolos Colectivos*, translated by Jesus Casquete y Josetxo Beriain, Círculo Eranos I, 135-219 (Barcelona: Anthropos, 1994).

Swedish

*Sw*A64 *Självmordet och själen.* Translated by Gudrun Ullman. Stockholm: Rabén och Sjägren, 1967.

DUNQUIN SERIES

Rare monographs and translations, on psychology, mythology, and the classics, published by Spring Publications. (Dunquin, an Irish peninsula pointing across the Atlantic toward America, lies at the farthest fringe of European civilization.)

For more information contact:
Spring Publications
299 East Quassett Road
Woodstock, Connecticut 06281
http://www.neca.com/~spring